I0413237

USGS Exploration Geochemistry Studies at the Pebble Porphyry Cu-Au-Mo Deposit, Alaska—PDF of Presentation

By Robert G. Eppinger, Karen D. Kelley, David L. Fey, Stuart A. Giles, Burke J. Minsley, and Steven M. Smith

Open-File Report 2010–1225

U.S. Department of the Interior
U.S. Geological Survey

U.S. Department of the Interior
KEN SALAZAR, Secretary

U.S. Geological Survey
Marcia K. McNutt, Director

U.S. Geological Survey, Reston, Virginia: 2010

For product and ordering information:
World Wide Web: http://www.usgs.gov/pubprod
Telephone: 1-888-ASK-USGS

For more information on the USGS—the Federal source for science about the Earth,
its natural and living resources, natural hazards, and the environment:
World Wide Web: http://www.usgs.gov
Telephone: 1-888-ASK-USGS

Suggested citation:
Eppinger, R.G., Kelley, K.D., Fey, D.L., Giles, S.A., Minsley, B.J., and Smith, S.M., 2010, USGS exploration
geochemistry studies at the Pebble porphyry Cu-Au-Mo deposit, Alaska—pdf of presentation: U.S.
Geological Survey Open-File Report 2010–1225, 64 p.

Introduction

From 2007 through 2010, scientists in the U.S. Geological Survey (USGS) have been conducting exploration-oriented geochemical and geophysical studies in the region surrounding the giant Pebble porphyry Cu-Au-Mo deposit in southwestern Alaska. The Cretaceous Pebble deposit is concealed under tundra, glacial till, and Tertiary cover rocks, and is undisturbed except for numerous exploration drill holes. These USGS studies are part of a nation-wide research project on evaluating and detecting concealed mineral resources. This report focuses on exploration geochemistry and comprises illustrations and associated notes that were presented as a case study in a workshop on this topic. The workshop, organized by L.G. Closs and R. Glanzman, is called "Geochemistry in Mineral Exploration and Development," presented by the Society of Economic Geologists at a technical conference entitled "The Challenge of Finding New Mineral Resources: Global Metallogeny, Integrative Exploration and New Discoveries," held at Keystone, Colorado, October 2–5, 2010.

USGS Exploration Geochemistry Studies at the Pebble Porphyry Cu-Au-Mo Deposit, Alaska

Robert G. Eppinger, Karen D. Kelley, David L. Fey, Stuart A. Giles, Burke Minsley, and Steven M. Smith

In 2007, the USGS began a collaborative research project with Northern Dynasty Minerals (now the Pebble Limited Partnership, PLP) to conduct studies at Pebble that are designed to develop or enhance exploration techniques (largely geochemical and geophysical) to identify mineralized rock beneath cover.

THANKS!

Pebble Limited Partnership (Northern Dynasty, Inc. and Anglo American LLC)

Lena Brommeland
Sean Magee
Keith Roberts
Gernot Wober

Jim Lang
Mark Rebagliati
Robin Smith
and others!

Analytical Laboratories

Acme Labs
ALS Chemex
Skyline Labs

Activation Labs
SGS Minerals
USGS

Our studies would not be possible without support from the companies and people listed here. The PLP is providing logistical support in the form of helicopter support, room and board, and so forth, as well as scientific input. Analytical labs provided geochemical analyses using exotic techniques not commonly in use by the USGS to showcase their methods.

Studies Underway

USGS:

- ❖ Exploration Geochemistry (soil, water, sediment)

- ❖ Porphyry Cu Indicator Minerals (PCIMs)

- ❖ Geophysics (regional and deposit scale)

Mineral Resources Program External Grants:

- ❖ Lithogeochemical/isotopic study to discriminate barren versus fertile igneous phases

- ❖ Thermal history and post-mineralization landscape evolution (low temperature apatite fission track and apatite U-Th/He methods)

These are the various aspects of our studies. I will only be touching upon the first two of these. The last two are currently underway and are being conducted in collaboration with scientists from academia and with the mining company; results are preliminary.

This is a view of most of the deposit, looking NW. Edge to edge scale in the center of the photo is about 2 km.

Note covered terrane and glacial features.

Brief exploration history:

1) Pebble West (PW) was discovered in 1989 by Cominco America following up a color anomaly identified by a pilot.

2) Since 2001, Northern Dynasty Minerals (NDM) has explored the area, resulting in the discovery of Pebble East (PE) in 2005.

3) In July 2007, NDM partnered with Anglo American in a joint venture to advance the project.

4) The combined resource is indicated on the slide.

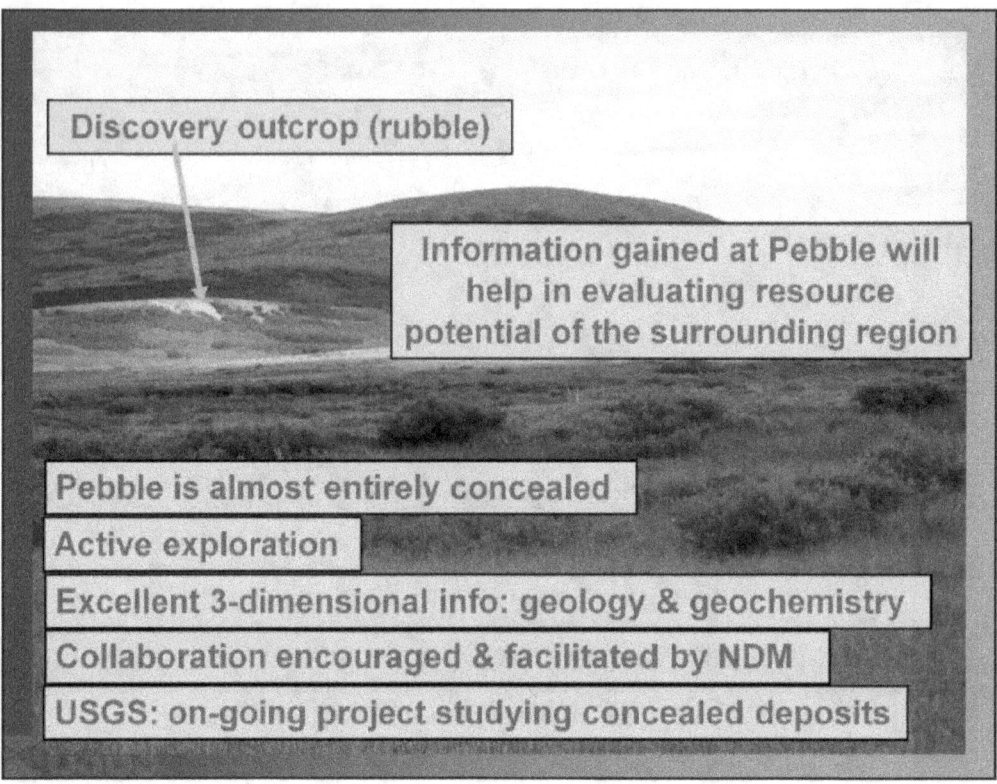

Here is a view of the Discovery outcrop.

Reasons why USGS chose Pebble for study:

The remainder covered. Explain that the covered nature and active exploration (excellent three dimensional information with all the drilling) made this is ideal place for the USGS to collaborate with the company to conduct investigations to identify techniques that can be used to assess the resource at depth.

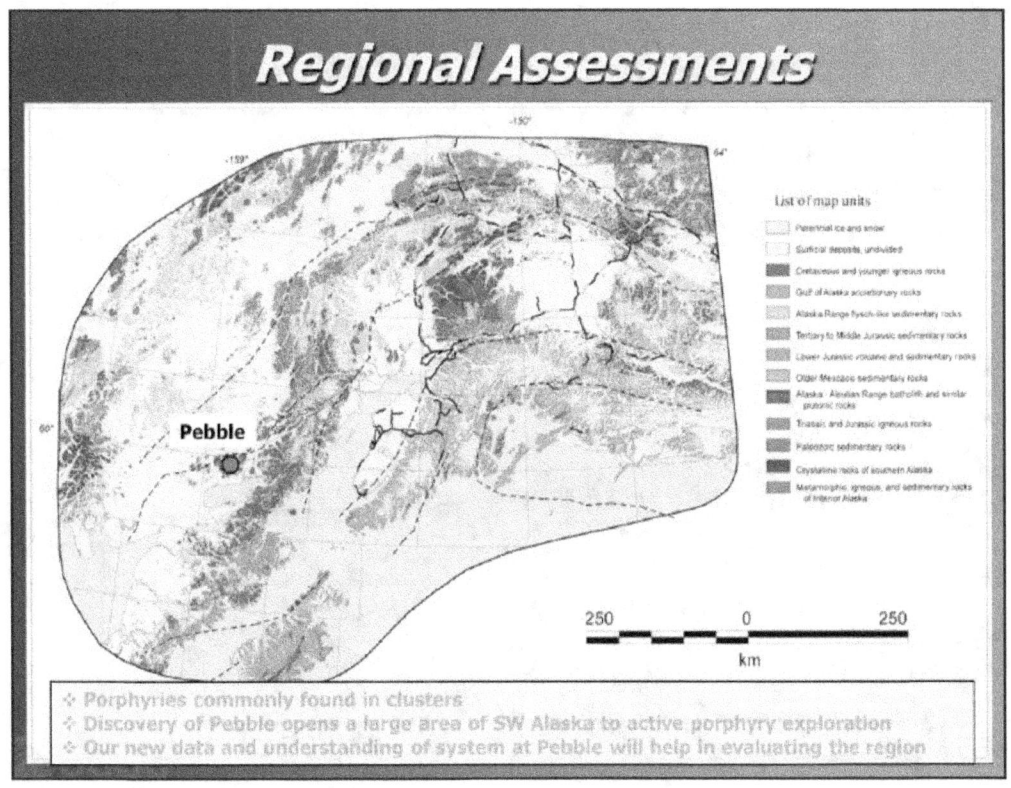

This regional geology compilation from Ric Wilson (USGS) indicates the extent of cover in the region.

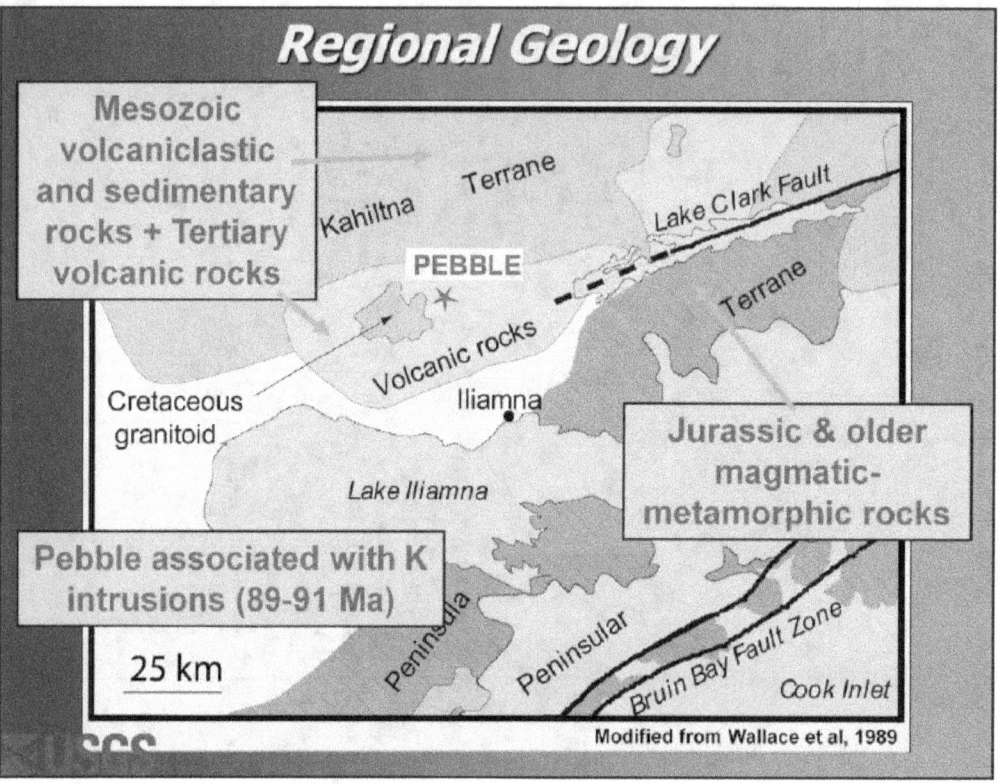

The Pebble deposit is located in the southern Kahiltna terrane, near the boundary between two lithologic packages:

1) An assemblage of Mesozoic volcaniclastic and sedimentary rocks overlain by Tertiary volcanic rocks to the northwest and Jurassic and older magmatic-metamorphic rocks to the southeast.

2) The Lake Clark fault is coincident with the lithologic change.

3) Intrusions of diverse composition and age occur along a northeast-trending corridor.

4) Pebble is associated with Cretaceous age intrusions (89 to 91 Ma).

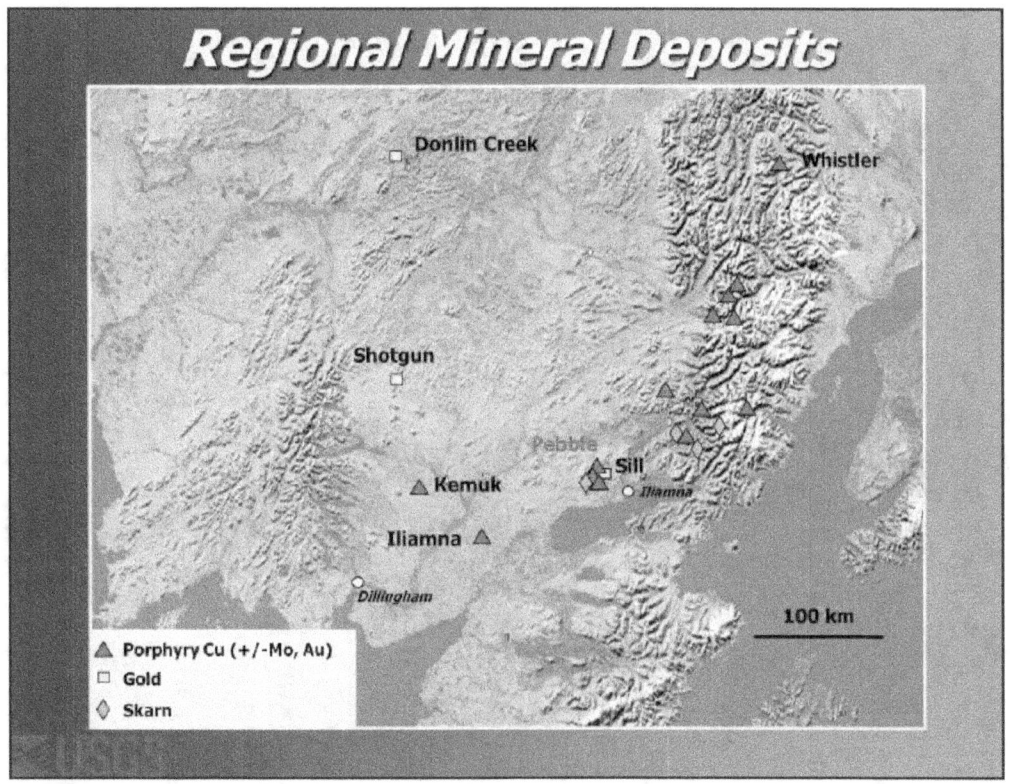

This map shows the distribution of known skarn, porphyry, and gold deposits in the region.

Porphyry deposits to the northeast of Pebble are generally younger than Pebble.

In the Pebble district, additional porphyry, skarn, and epithermal deposits have been identified.

The Kemuk and Iliamna porphyry occurrences to the southwest are also completely concealed by glacial and/or young volcanic rocks.

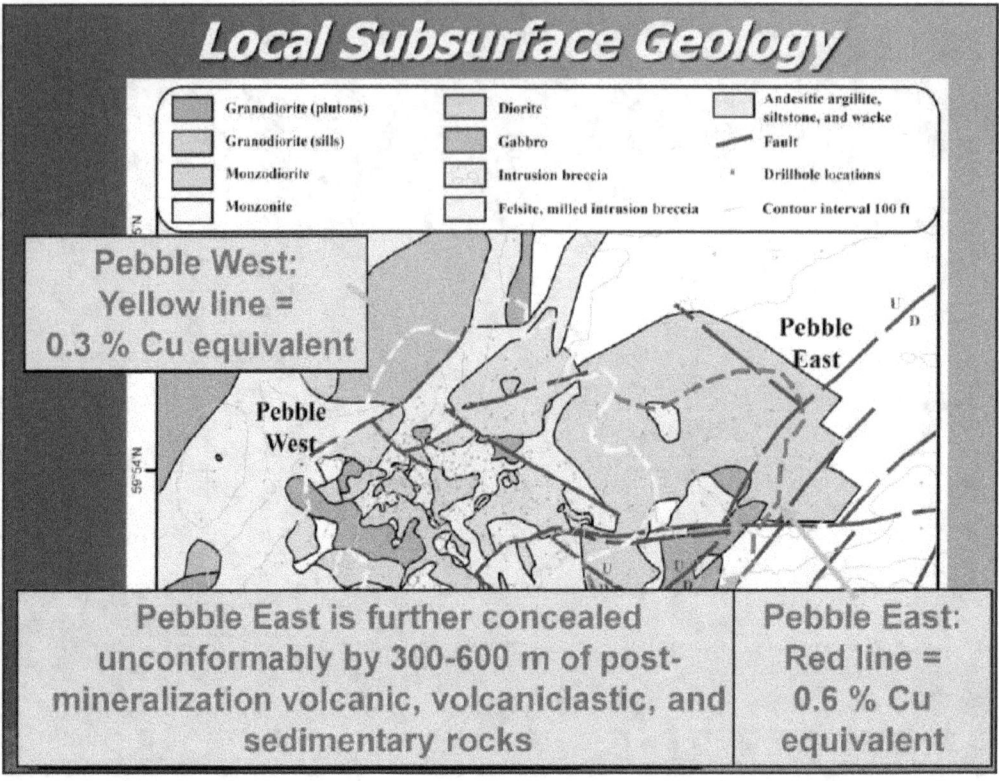

This is subsurface geology with drillholes indicated by small gray dots.

1) Pebble deposit consists of two main zones: the Pebble West outline is in yellow and the Pebble East outline is in red.

2) Mineralization and alteration are associated with multiple phases of quartz vein and stockworks in/around granodiorite stocks and sills.

3) The West zone occurs in small granodiorite stocks and in the wall rocks above and on the flanks of the intrusion.

4) The Pebble East deposit occurs in a large granodiorite stock and includes continuous mineralized rock over vertical lengths exceeding 700 meters.

5) PE cut off by graben-bounding faults.

6) Entire area is covered by glacial deposits up to 50 m thick.

7) Over Pebble East, the glacial deposits overlie about 300–600 m of post-mineralization volcanic, volcaniclastic, and sedimentary rocks that unconformably overlie Pebble East.

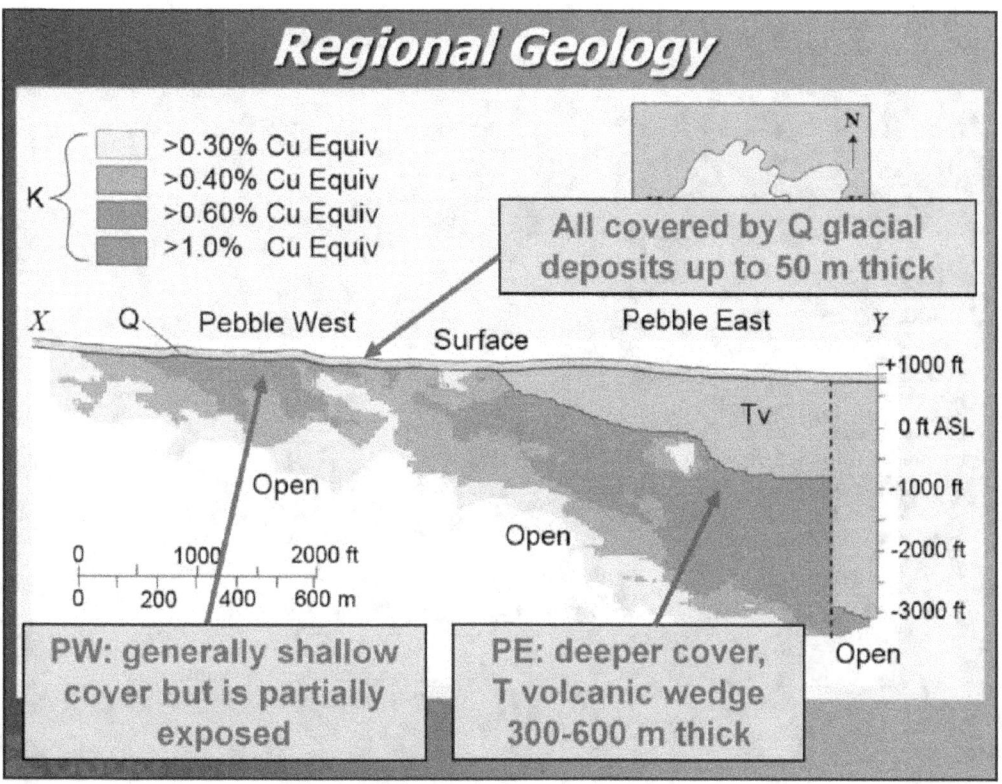

This stylized cross section shows how Pebble West is concealed by thin cover, whereas Pebble East is much deeper under cover.

The graben-bounding faults at the east edge of Pebble East are also stylized here.

Ore grades are significantly higher at Pebble East, which remains open at depth.

Mineralized rock is found in granodiorite and the surrounding sediments. Sulfides occur mostly in strong K-silicate alteration dominated by K-feldspar with highly variable biotite.

Chalcopyrite, molybdenite, and accessory pyrite occur as disseminations or in multi-generation stockworks of quartz-carbonate-sulfide veins.

Gold occurs mainly within chalcopyrite. Abundant high-grade bornite-bearing mineralized rock occurs in the core of Pebble East.

Exploration Geochemistry

Sample Media

- ❖ Surface and groundwater
- ❖ Soils (various horizons) using a variety of leach extractions and analytical methods
- ❖ Indicator Minerals in glacial till
- ❖ Pond sediments
- ❖ Vegetation (alder, willow, bog birch)
- ❖ Stream sediments/heavy mineral concentrates

We have experimented with a wide variety of exploration geochemical techniques to identify what works best for delineating both shallow and deep Pebble mineralized zones.

I'll first talk about the water, then the soil, and finally the indicator mineral studies.

Because of time constraints, I won't describe here our work related to the vegetation or stream sediments analyses.

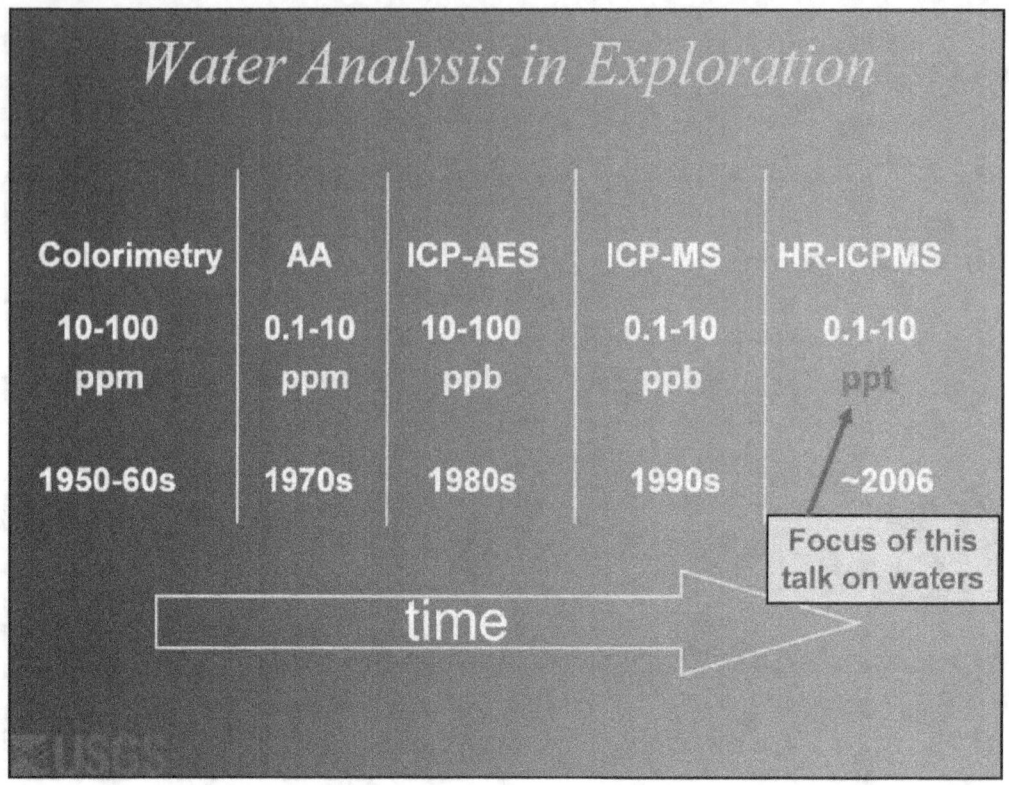

Lower determination limits for water samples have progressed from the ppm (mg/L) range in the 1970s and before, to the ppb (µg/L) range in the 1980s through the present.

Around 2006, high–resolution ICPMS became commercially available, and lowered determination limits by another couple of orders of magnitude, down to the ppt (ng/L) range.

For the water data, I will focus on the high–resolution ICPMS data.

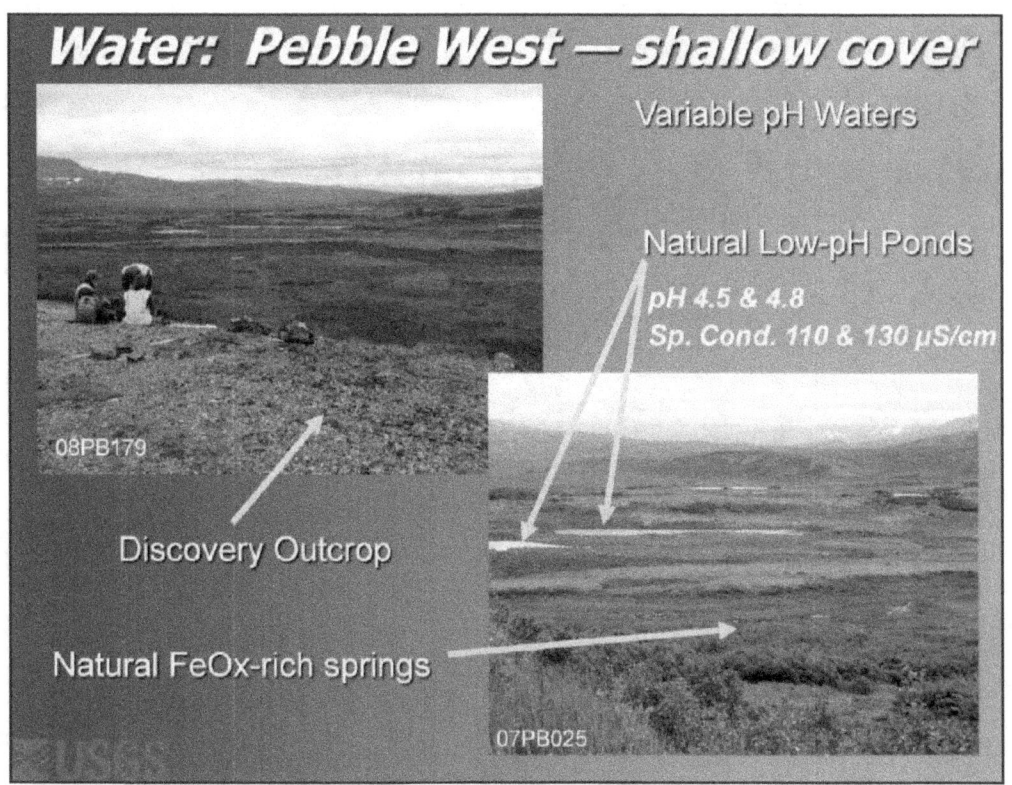

A small part of the deposit is exposed at Pebble West.

Natural FeOx-rich springs and low-pH ponds are present in this area.

Water: Pebble East — thick cover

Circum-Neutral Waters

Underlain by major
NE-trending faults

pH 6.5
cond. 12
µS/cm
08PB140

pH 6.8
cond. 75
µS/cm
08PB202

Here are a couple of ponds from the Pebble East area.

Waters at Pebble East are all circum-neutral in pH.

A series of major NE-trending faults underlie the eastern part of this area.

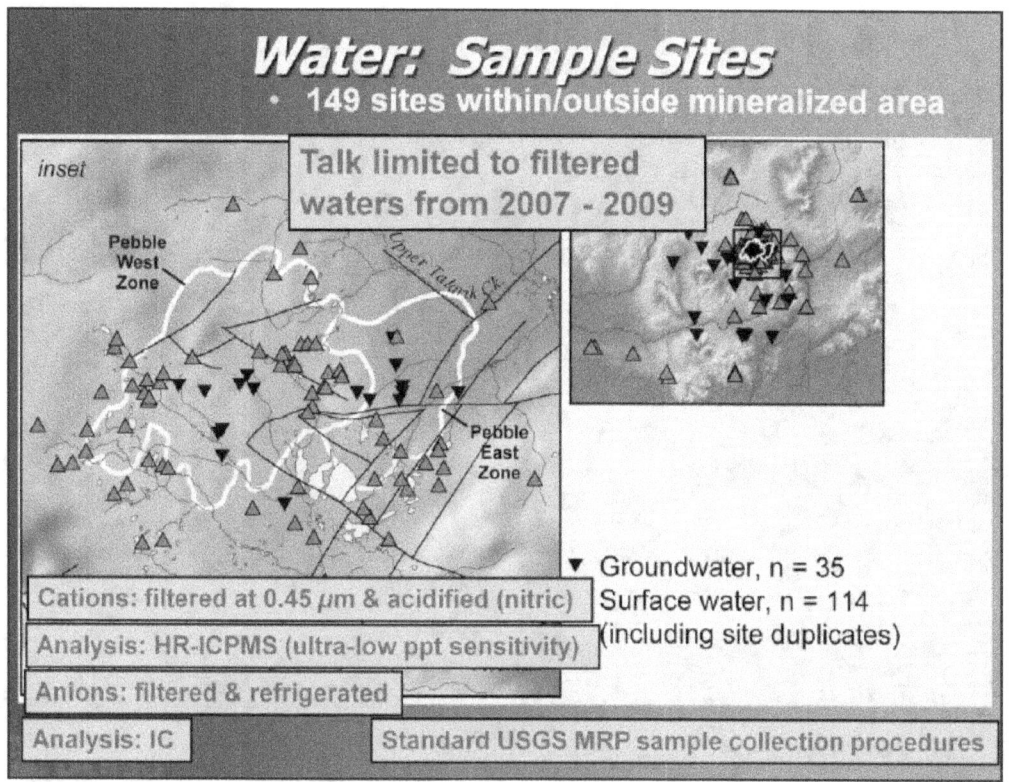

Pond–, spring–, and stream–water samples were collected at 149 sites (including site duplicates) within and outside the mineralized zone.

We collected both filtered and unfiltered samples: however, I'll only discuss the filtered samples.

Waters: quality control

07PB088

- Always a critical component, but especially with low ppt sensitivity

- Field blanks, site duplicates, analytical duplicates, standards

- Comprised about 15 % of samples

- Results:
  - No contamination by sample processing
  - Blanks—low concentrations of majors (< 5 ppb)
  - Blanks—most trace elements not detected (ppt)
  - Site duplicates—within ± 20% for most; ± 10% for some elements (even at low ppt levels, except when near DL)
  - SRMs—good to ± 10% for most elements
- Caution: Many SRMs do not have certified values for some elements that occur at the low concentrations detectable by HR-ICPMS

Sample collection for Hg analysis

Considering the ultra-low ppt determination limits available by HR-ICPMS, many SRMs do not have certified values for some elements that occur at the low concentrations detectable by this new method.

Data precision can be addressed for these elements and is generally good (site duplicates are within ± 20 percent for most and ± 10 percent for some elements).

However, new standards need to be developed to address the absolute accuracy of the data for some trace elements. This is a natural evolution for new analytical techniques with ever-lower determination limits.

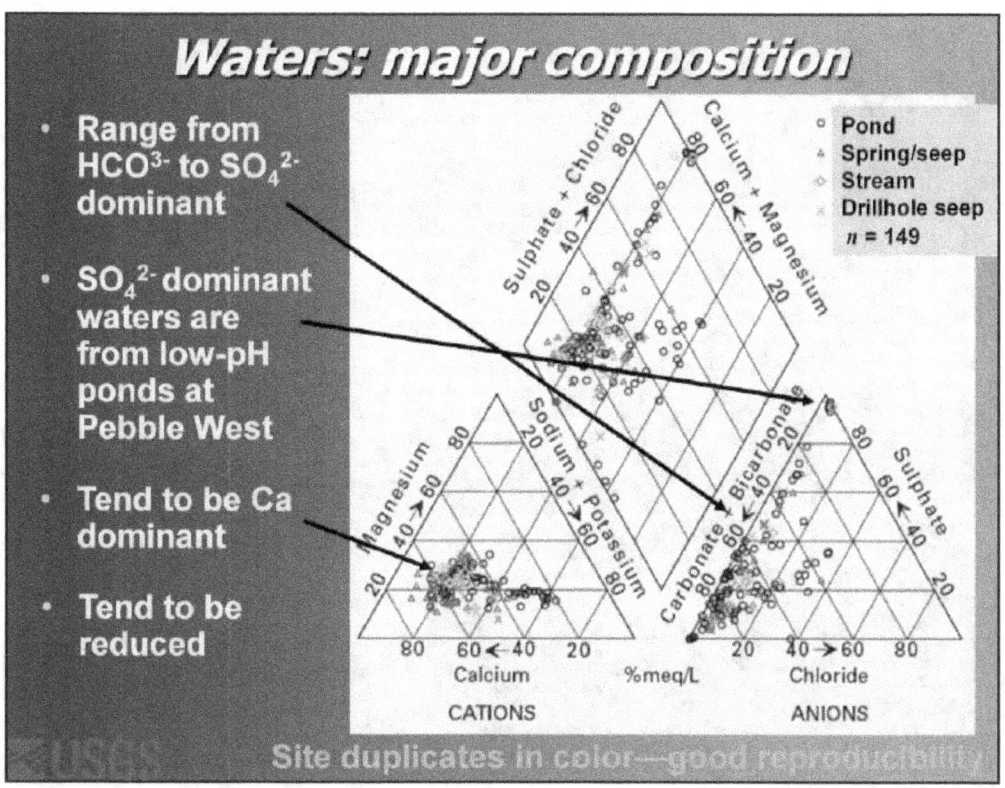

Now I'll discuss some aspects of the surface–water chemistry.

This Piper plot shows the major composition of the water samples.

Sample site duplicates are shown in color pairs.

The duplicate pairs essentially plot on top of one another, indicating minimal combined site + analytical error.

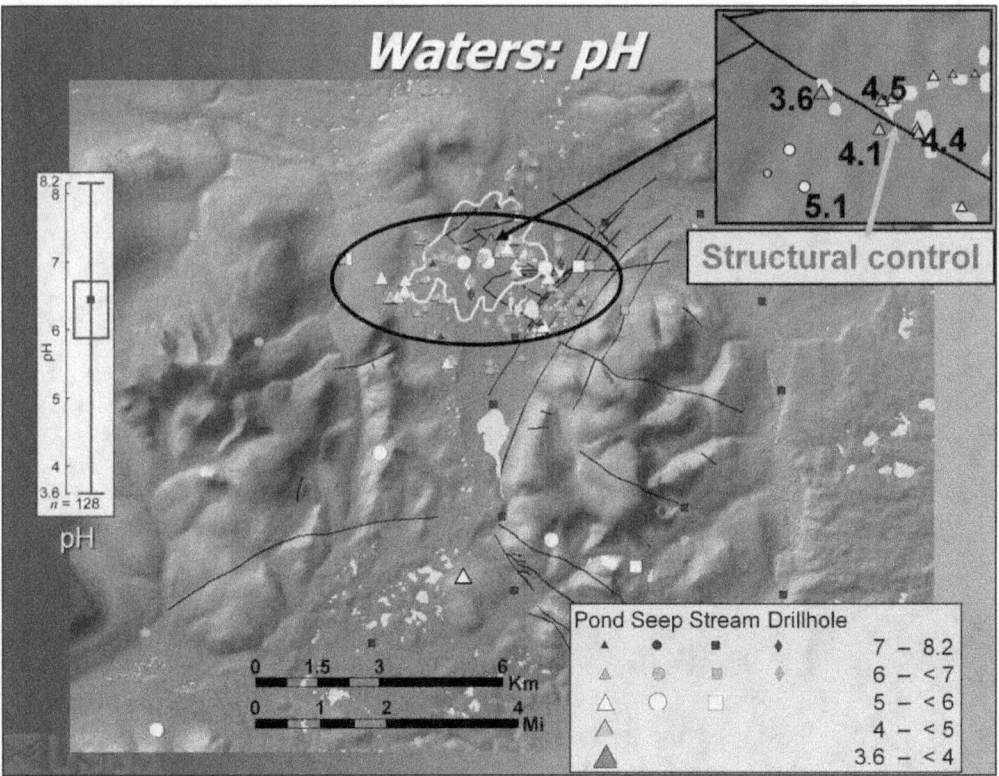

Median water pH is 6.4; most values are at or above 6.

In the Pebble area proper, there is a cluster of ponds and seeps with pH values between 5 and 6 (yellow).

The lowest pH values in the entire study area, all below 5, are found in four ponds near exposed mineralized rock at Pebble West, aligned along a NW-trending fault.

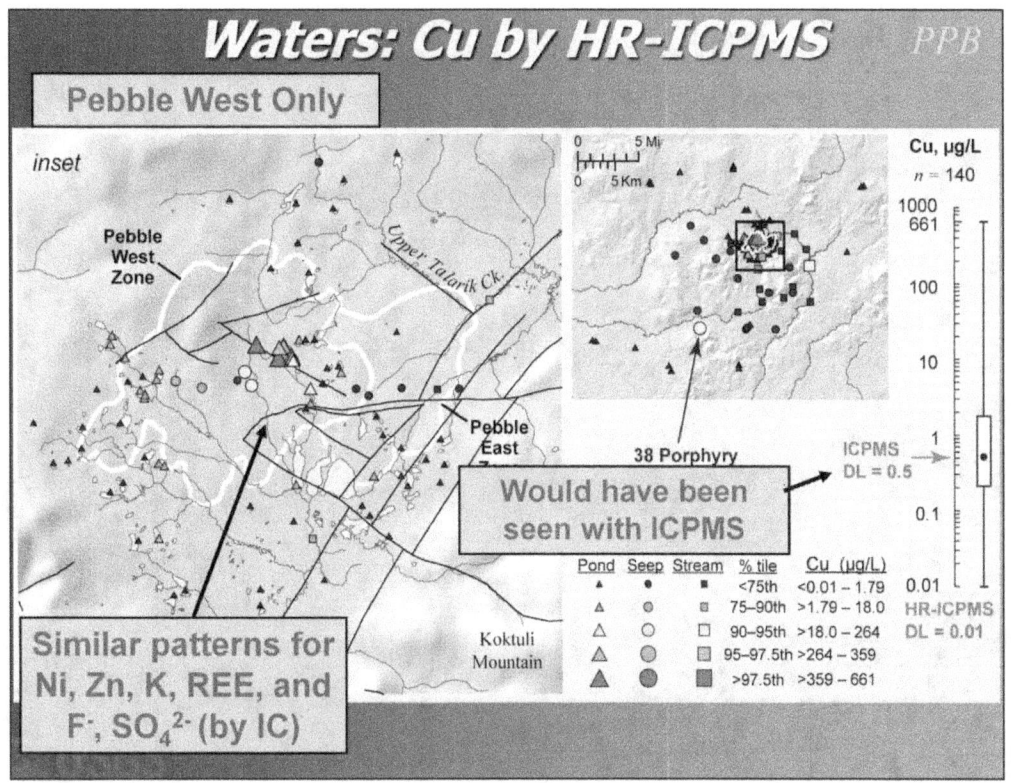

Now we'll look at some maps showing Pebble West results.

Units switch from ppb to ppt, so keep an eye on the upper right corner of the slide.

In the next several slides, the lower determination limits for both ICPMS and HR-ICPMS are shown in red.

For copper, an anomalous cluster of ponds and springs with concentrations in the high 10s to 100s of ppb range is evident around the low–pH ponds near the exposed part of Pebble West (yellows, oranges, and reds in slide).

There are also numerous low-level anomalous samples in low 10s of ppb in near-neutral pH ponds to south and west.

The low-pH ponds contain high concentrations of several other elements including Ni, Zn, K, the REE, and also in F- and SO4^{2-} by ion chromatography.

pH appears to be a dominant control.

The 38 Porphyry zone (inset map), a small concealed Cu porphyry occurrence, is also identified by these data.

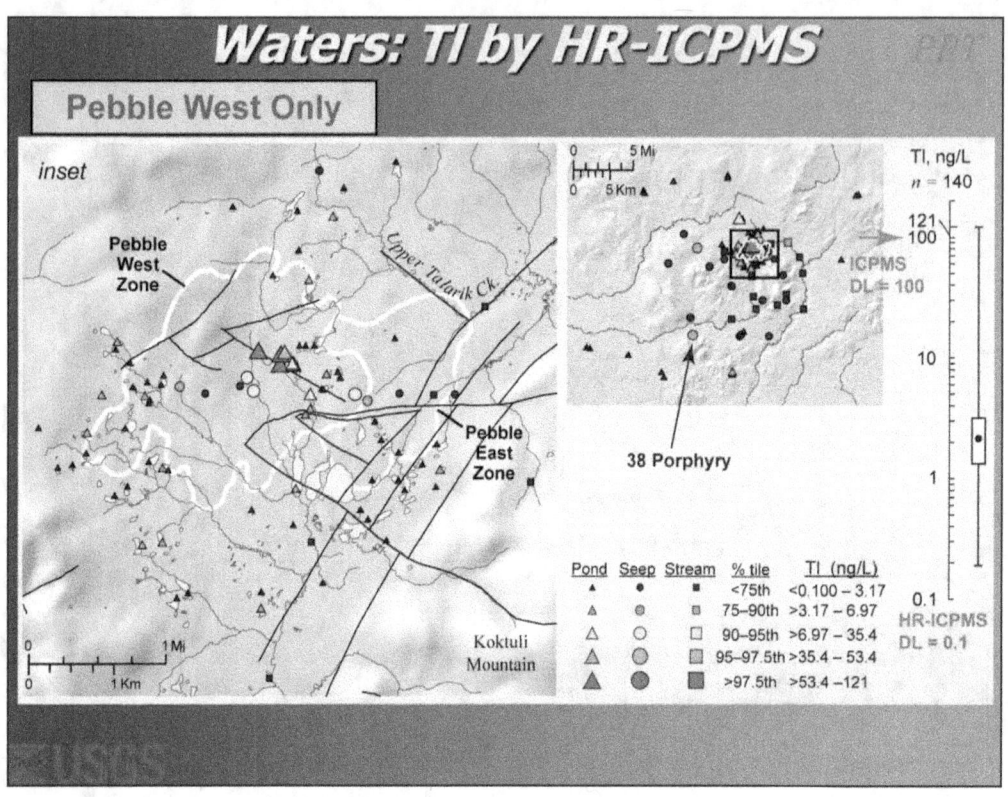

Thallium by HR-ICPMS highlights the same low-pH ponds and springs, but at low ppt levels.

Less-anomalous samples form a broad halo around Pebble West.

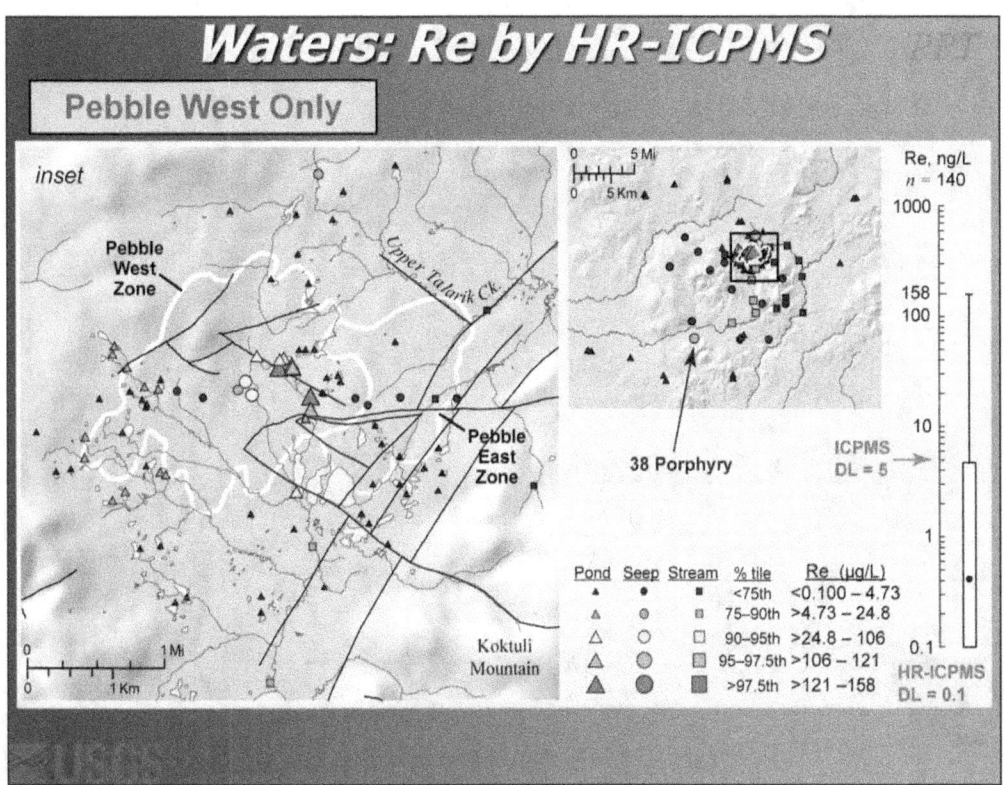

Rhenium by HR-ICPMS highlights these same ponds and springs, but at low ppt levels.

Less-anomalous samples form a broad halo around Pebble West.

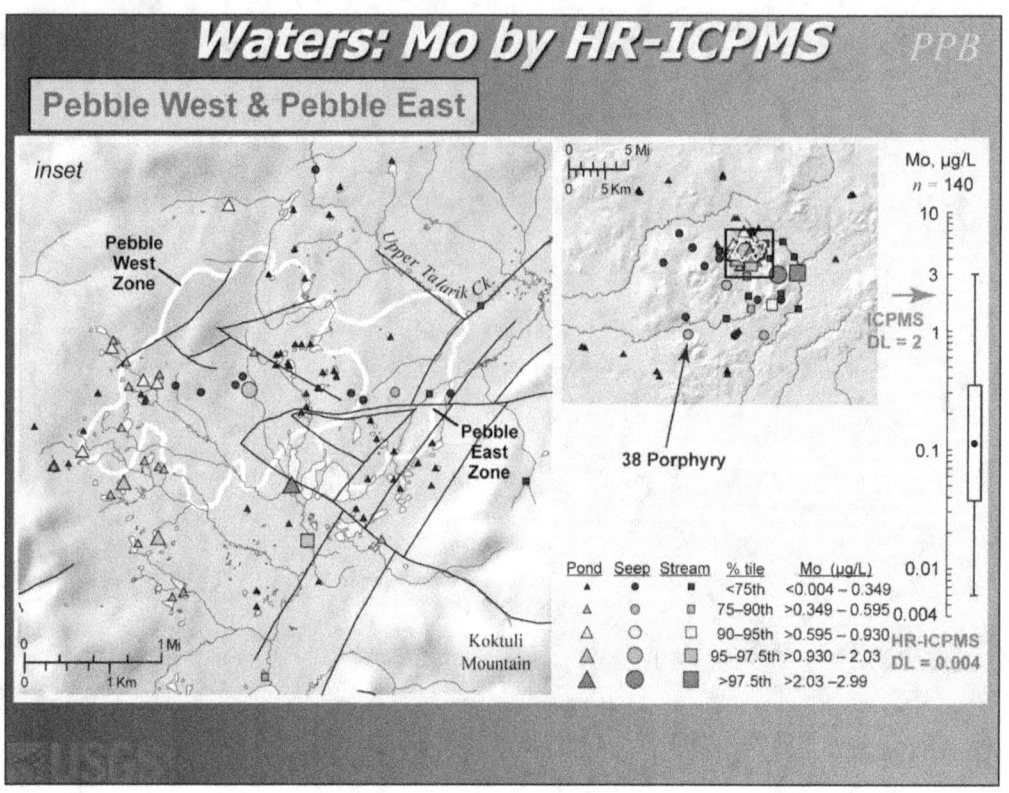

Now we'll look at a few elements that highlight both Pebble West and Pebble East.

For molybdenum, a large cluster of anomalous ponds and springs covering several square kilometers occur around both Pebble West and East.

Isolated anomalous samples are also present on east side of Koktuli Mountain.

Though low in absolute magnitude, these concentrations are well-above the HR-ICPMS detection limit.

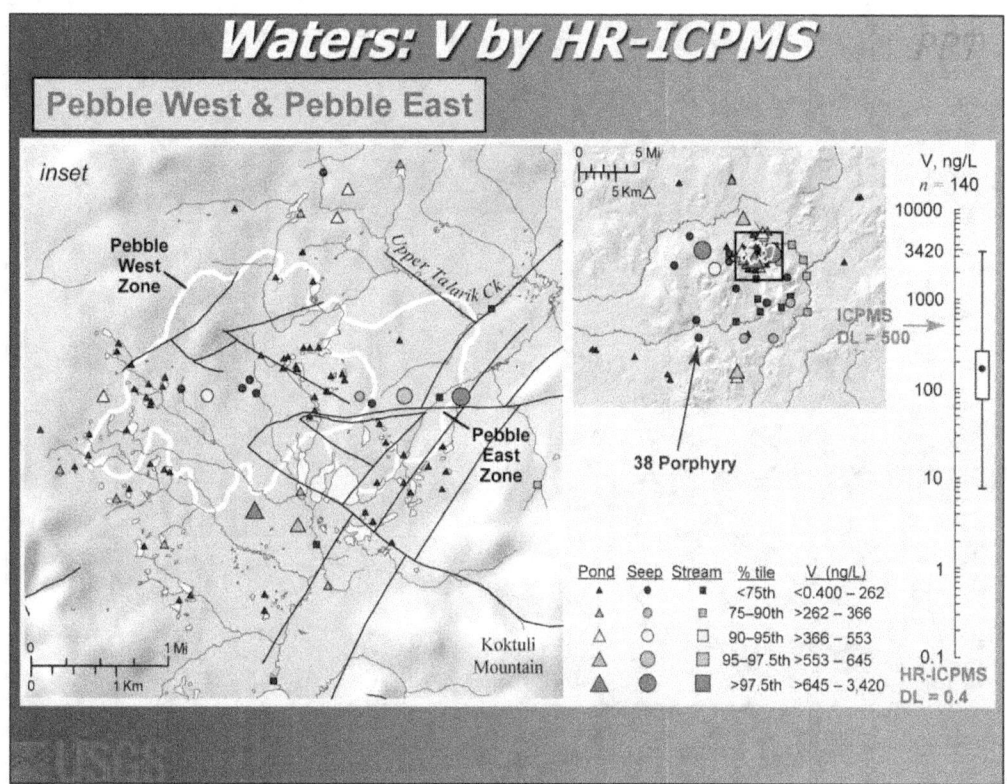

Ponds and springs from a broad area around Pebble West and East contain anomalous vanadium, generally at hundreds of ppt levels.

You might even imagine seeing some dispersion down Talarik Creek to the east, although that is conjectural (smaller map, right side).

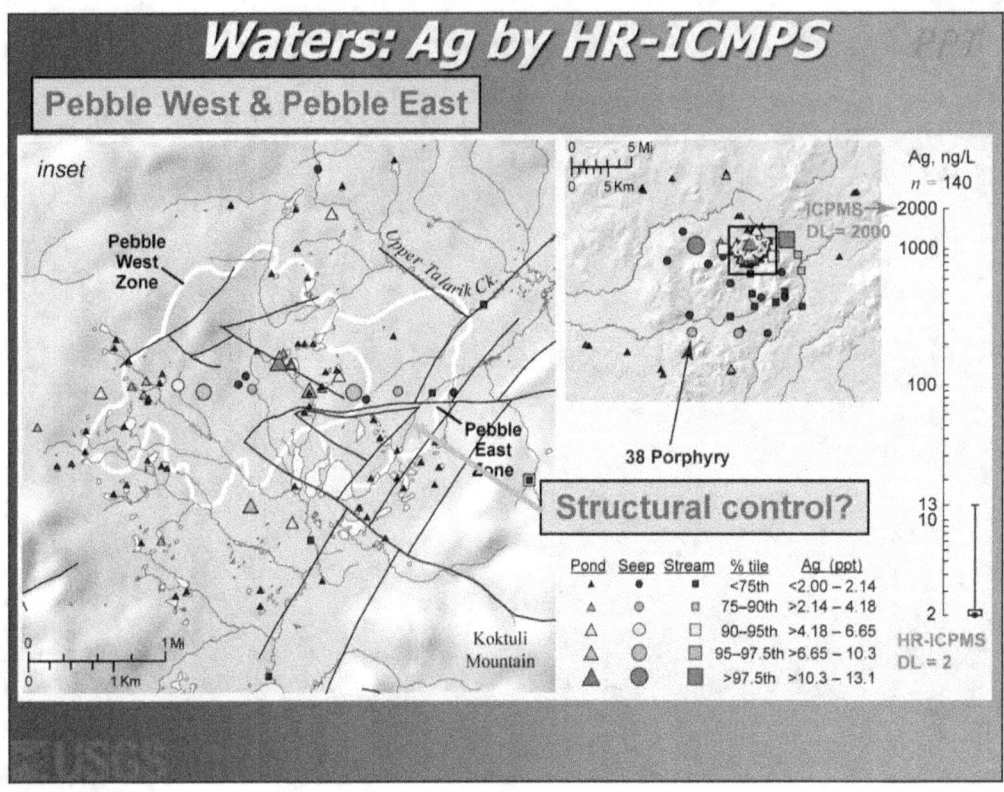

For silver, a large cluster of anomalous ponds and springs is present around Pebble, but at exceedingly low concentrations of 2 to 13 parts per trillion.

The majority of the data are non-detects.

Although caution is warranted because the values are close to the lower determination limit, the coherent pattern around Pebble is compelling.

A dispersion train may once again extend along Talarik Creek (smaller map, right side).

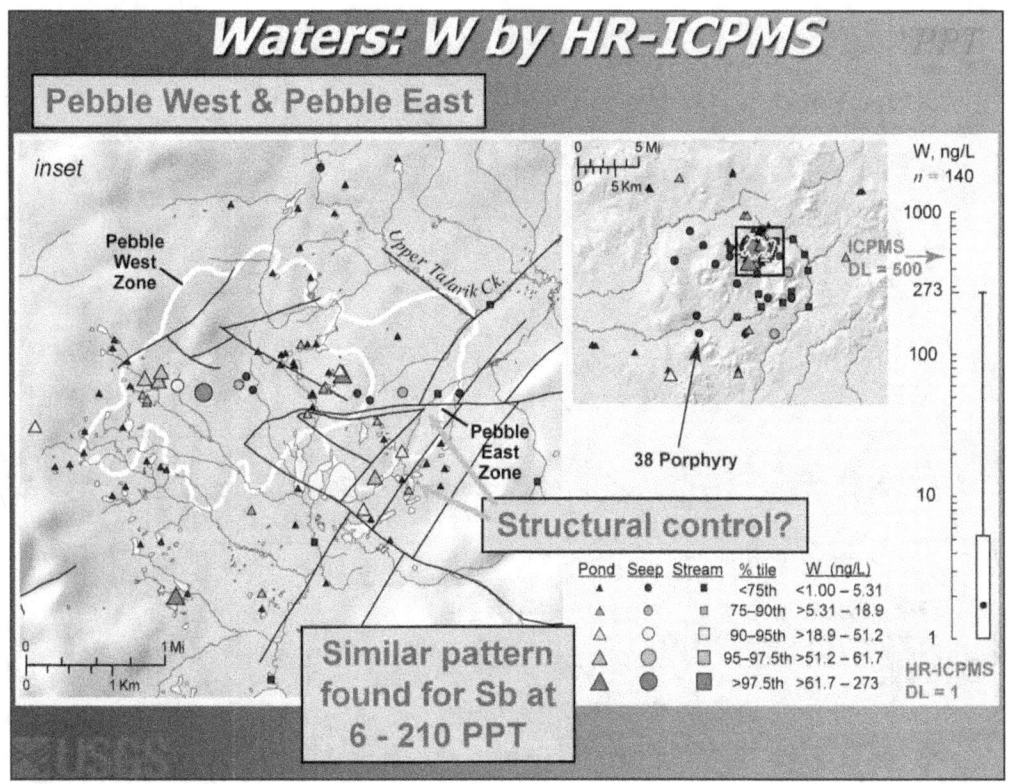

Here is tungsten showing anomalous values over both Pebble West and Pebble East.

At Pebble East, large NE-trending faults underlie the anomalous ponds.

Samples with anomalous Sb concentrations are similarly distributed.

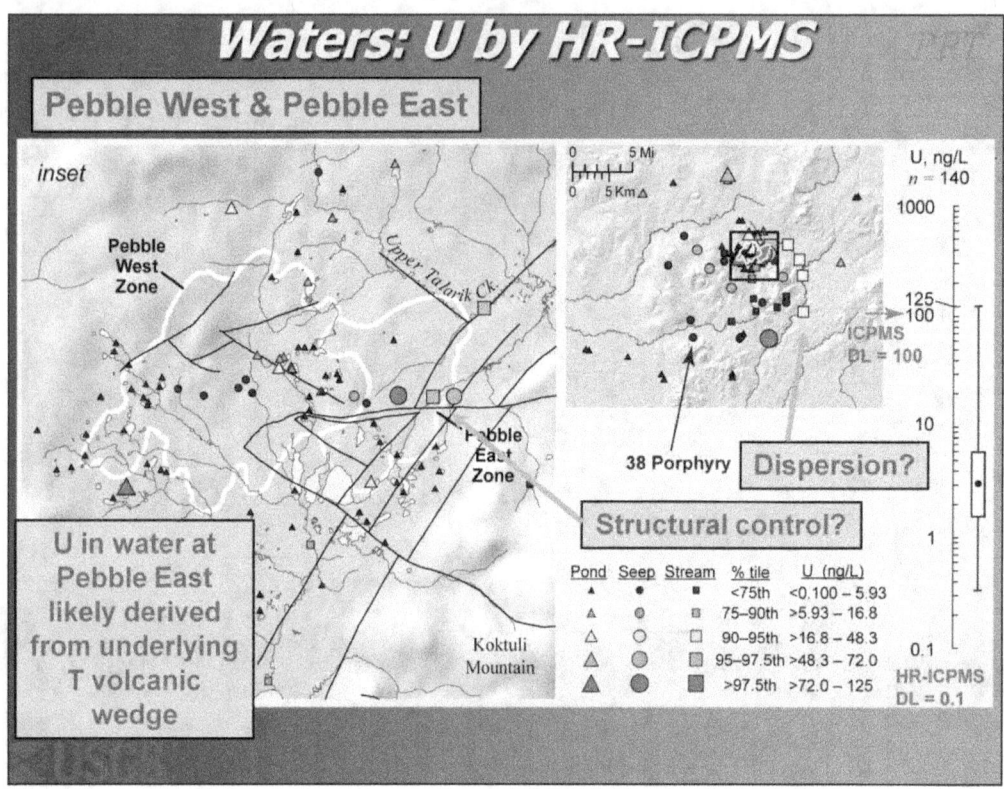

Ponds and springs overlying NE-trending fault at Pebble East contain the highest concentrations of uranium. However, the concentrations are very low, ranging from around 50 to 105 ng/L.

The highest value, 125 ng/L, is from the spring sample at the southern edge of the map.

In sampled drill core, U concentrations are highest in Tertiary volcanic rocks that overlie the deep Pebble East ore body.

Again, the distribution suggests structural control and possible dispersion along Talarik Creek.

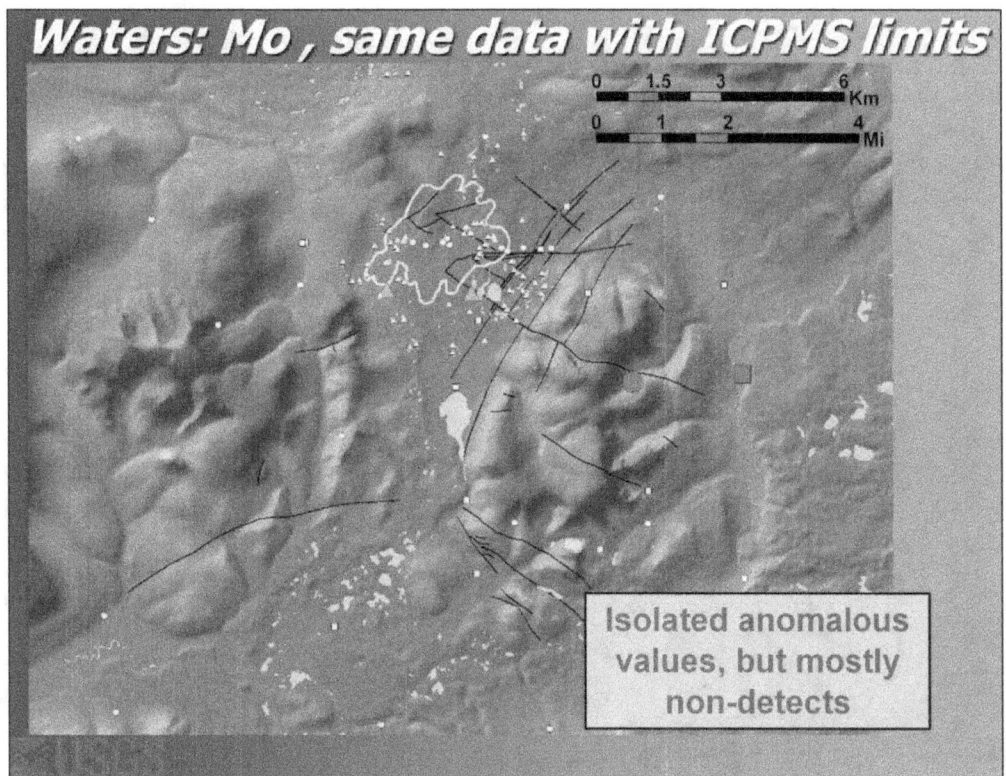

Waters: Mo , same data with ICPMS limits

Isolated anomalous values, but mostly non-detects

To illustrate the value of the HR-ICPMS data over traditional ICPMS, the following maps show the same data recast using ICPMS lower determination limits.

Mo was detected in only four samples, two at Pebble, and two along the eastern side of Koktuli Mountain.

All the other information is lost in non-detects.

I'll quickly show this same pattern for several elements.

Only the 2007–2008 data are shown here, not the 2009 data from more distal samples.

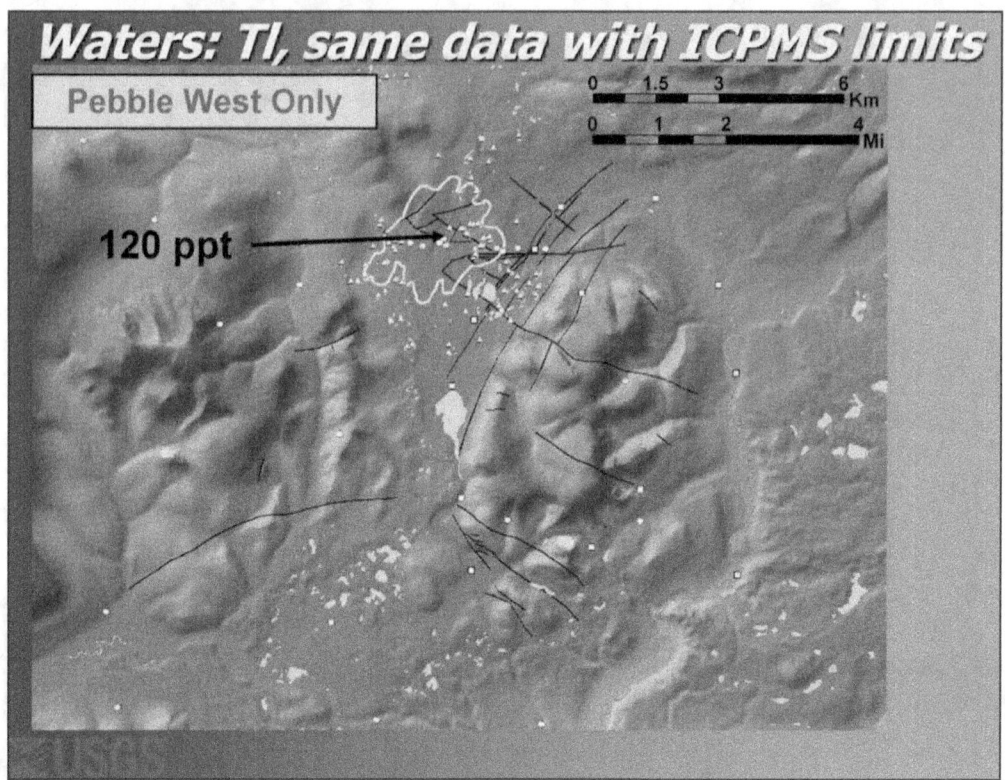

These are the same data recast using ICPMS detection limits.

Only one sample contains detectable Tl.

All other information is lost.

Only the 2007–2008 data are shown here, not the 2009 data from more distal samples.

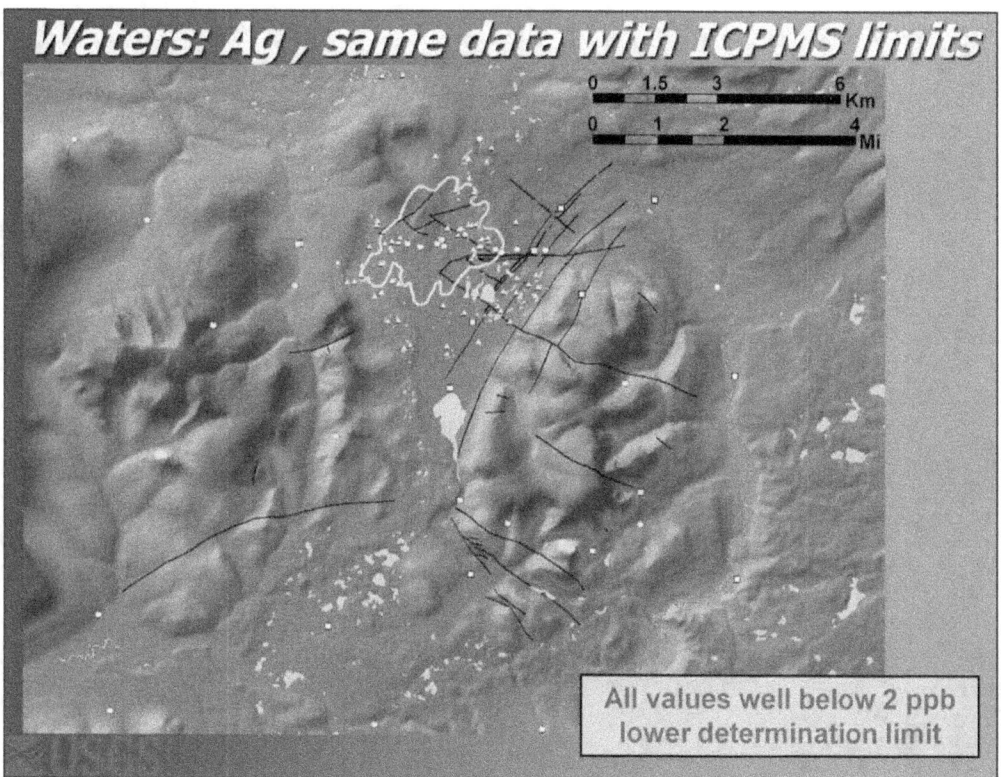

Waters: Ag , same data with ICPMS limits

All values well below 2 ppb lower determination limit

These are the same data recast using ICPMS detection limits.

All the information is lost in non-detects.

Only the 2007–2008 data are shown here, not the 2009 data from more distal samples.

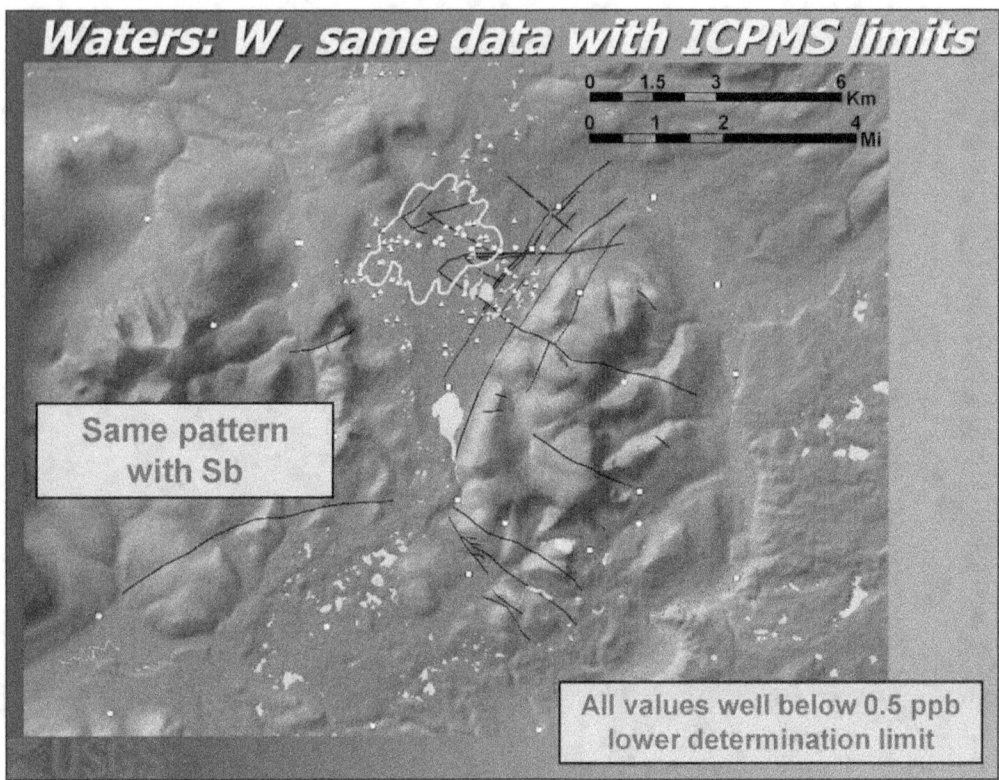

Waters: W , same data with ICPMS limits

Same pattern with Sb

All values well below 0.5 ppb lower determination limit

These are the same data recast using ICPMS detection limits.

All the information is lost in non-detects.

Sb shows this same pattern.

Only the 2007–2008 data are shown here, not the 2009 data from more distal samples.

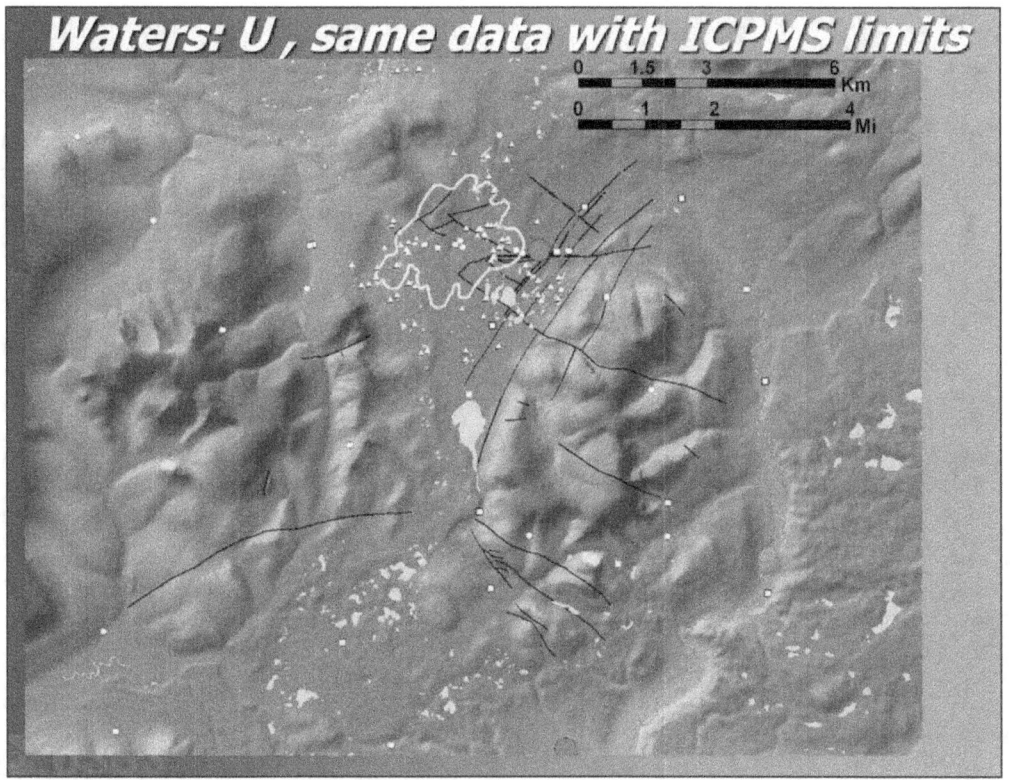

These are the same data recast using ICPMS detection limits.

Except for the two highest concentrations in spring samples, all the data are lost in non-detects.

Only the 2007–2008 data are shown here, not the 2009 data from more distal samples.

Waters: concluding remarks

- Pebble West: low pH-ponds contain anomalous concentrations of several elements at concentrations amenable to analysis by traditional ICPMS

- Pebble East: Low metals concentrations due to circum-neutral pH waters and depth of the ore body preclude use of traditional methods like ICPMS

- However, HR-ICPMS reveals several pathfinder elements and enlarges the target at both Pebble West and East

- Anomalies commonly coincide with underlying structures!

- **Caution:** Water sampling procedures for PPT-level analyses require strong QC program
  - "grab and run" sampling will likely result in false anomalies

- These data could be useful to establish baseline conditions

34

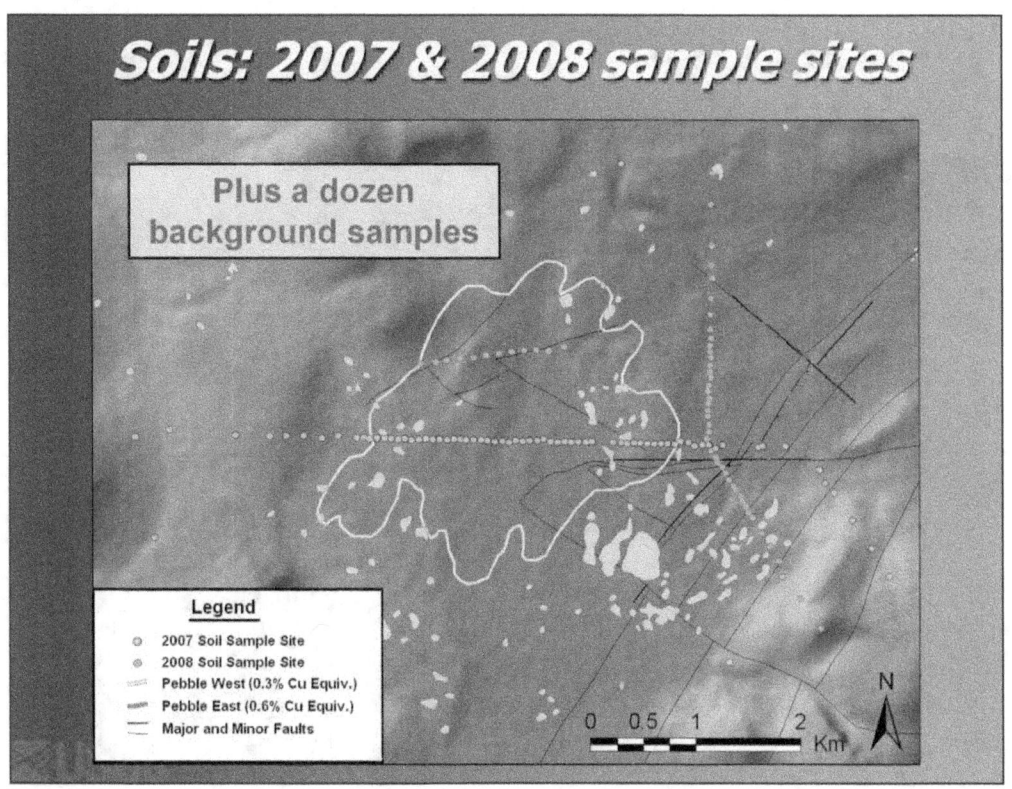

Soils were collected to test various partial extraction techniques.

Staggered spacing over deposit.

Plus about a dozen "background" samples.

I'll be showing cross sections along the E-W and N-S soil traverse lines.

Soils

Looking west across deposit

Approx. location of soil traverse

- Organic-rich A and B horizon soils were collected
- B horizon sieved to minus 80-mesh
- Samples analyzed for "totals" (4 acid digestion) and 10 different partial leach methods
- Total method: attacks sulfide phases
- Partial leaches: attack loosely bound metals in phases like Fe and Mn oxide coatings

A horizon

B horizon

At each soil site, we collected organic-rich A and B horizon samples.

We hypothesized that metals migrated for some distance upward to the sample site.

Aerial view of Pebble Deposit Area Looking NW

Pebble West   2007 Traverse   2008 Traverse   Pebble East

1.4 kilometer traverse
12 sites
4.5 kilometer traverse
44 sites
7.8 kilometer traverse
78 sites

In 2007, we collected soil samples from 78 sites along a 7.8–km east-west traverse across both the Pebble East and Pebble West zones.

In 2008, we added another 44 sites along a 4.5–km north-south traverse over the deeper Pebble East zone.

We also collected 12 sites from a short 1.4–km east-west traverse over an SP (self-potential) anomaly identified in the Pebble West zone.

At each site, a spade was used to dig a hole between 40 and 100 cm deep. A plastic scoop was then used to scrape the sides and clean out the hole.

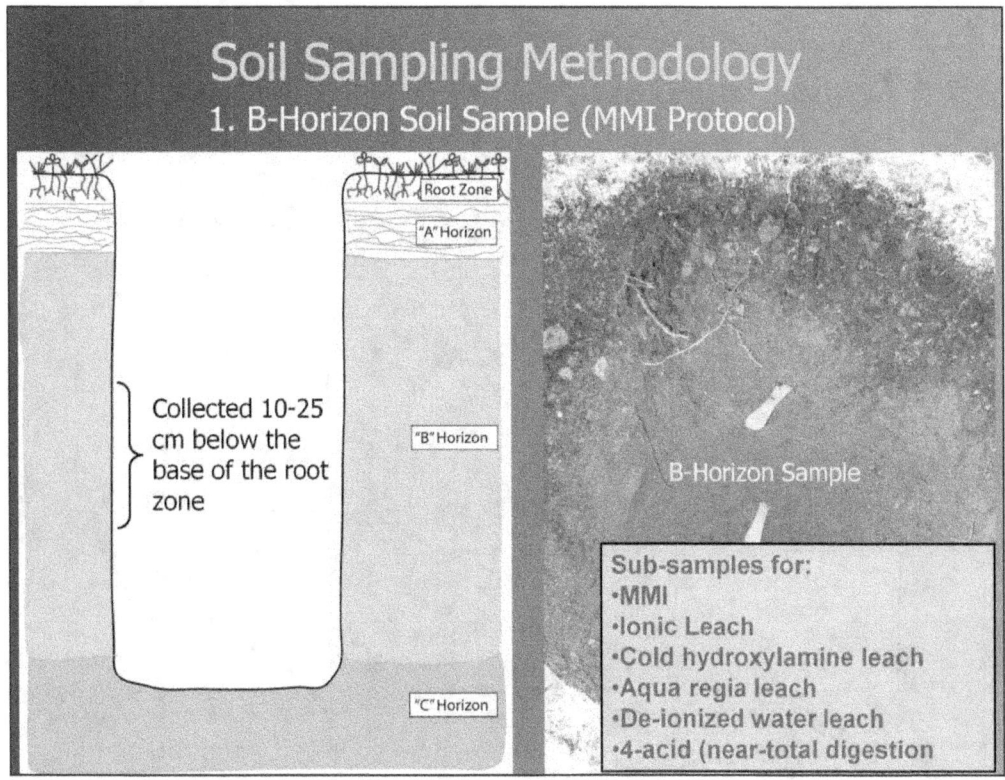

Four sub-samples were collected at each site. The first subsample was collected using the sampling protocol recommended for the Mobile Metal Ion (MMI) technique. The sampled material was a composite of soil collected 10–25 cm below the base of the root zone (usually in the B-horizon). Soil horizons were commonly poorly developed.

Note the sticks used to define the sampling interval in the hole.

This large sub-sample was split in the lab and analyzed by several leach techniques as indicated in slide. Only a few of these will be discussed here because of time constraints.

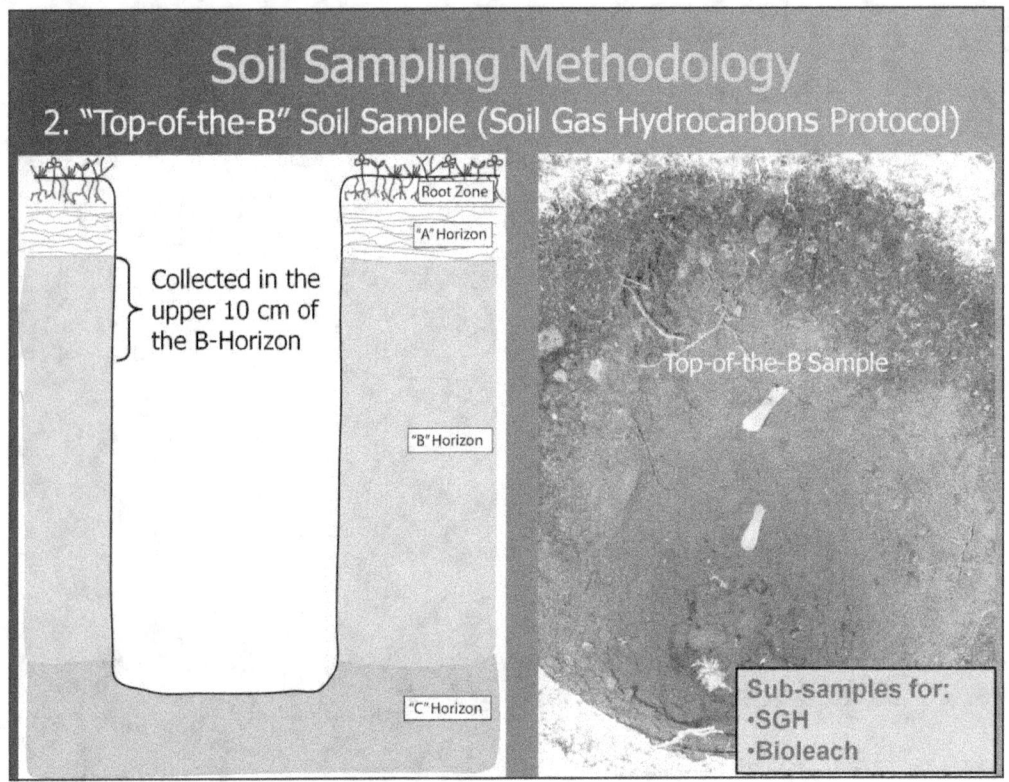

Soil Sampling Methodology
2. "Top-of-the-B" Soil Sample (Soil Gas Hydrocarbons Protocol)

The second sub-sample was collected using the sampling protocol recommended for the Soil Gas Hydrocarbons technique. The sampled material was taken from the upper 10 cm of the B-horizon.

Note sample location in the soil hole picture

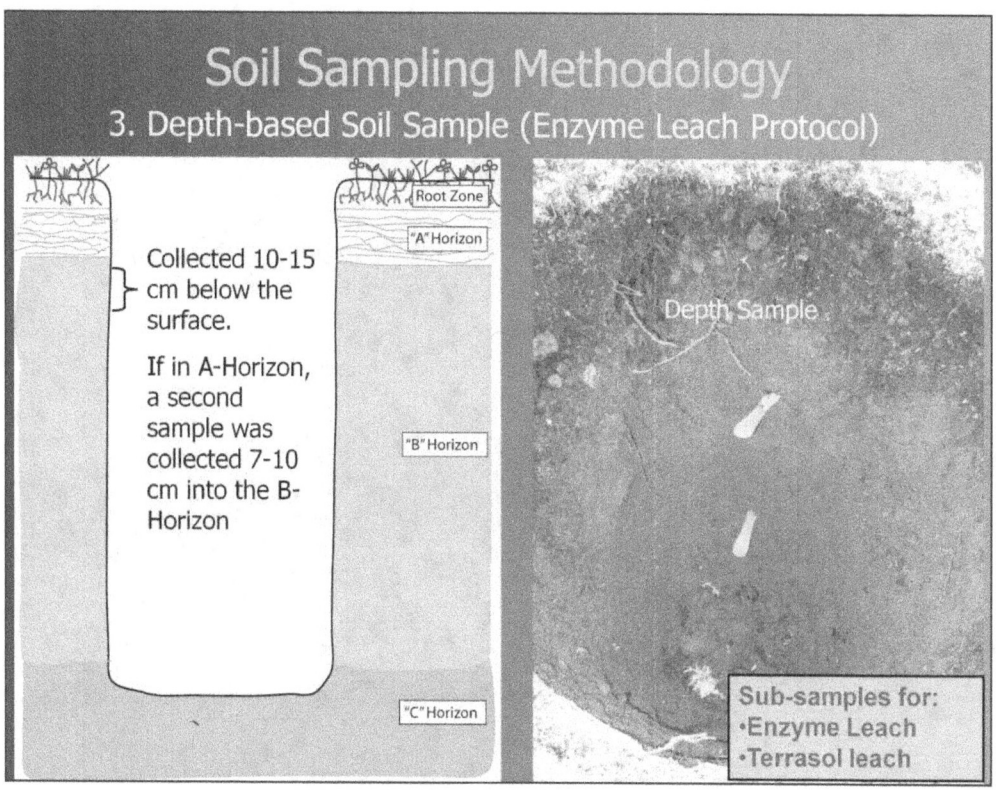

The third sub-sample was collected using the sampling protocol recommended for the Enzyme Leach technique. A 50-ml centrifuge tube was tightly packed with soil collected between 10 and 15 cm below the ground surface. If this sample was in the A-horizon, then a second centrifuge tube was filled with soil collected 7 to 10 cm into the B-horizon.

The fourth subsample was collected using the sampling protocol recommended for the Sodium Pyrophosphate Leach technique. Organic-rich soil was collected from the A-Horizon.

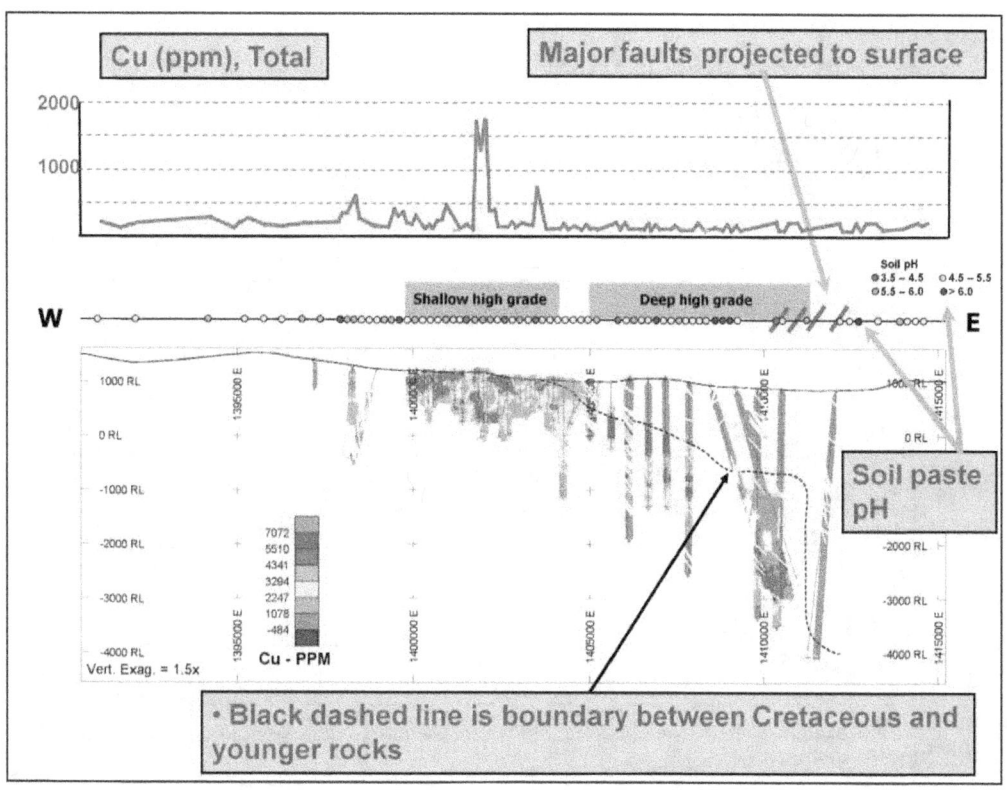

Now I'll show a few simplified geochemical cross sections.

Middle line: W–E soil traverse showing decreasing sample density moving away from deposit (60–m spacing over deposit, 150–m spacing near periphery, 300–m spacing more distal).

Soil paste pH is indicated by colored dots along soil traverse. The lowest pH values are red and yellow. Highest values are blues.

Bottom section: down-hole geologic and geochemical information from drill holes projected along the soil traverse. The black dotted line is the boundary between Cretaceous and younger rocks. Colors represent Cu contents in this particular case. The gray short lines along drill holes are logged faults. So for example, in Pebble East, you can see the abundance of faults in some drill holes corresponding to the plan map of northeast–trending normal faults.

Top panel: chemistry along soil traverse; in this case Cu by total analysis.

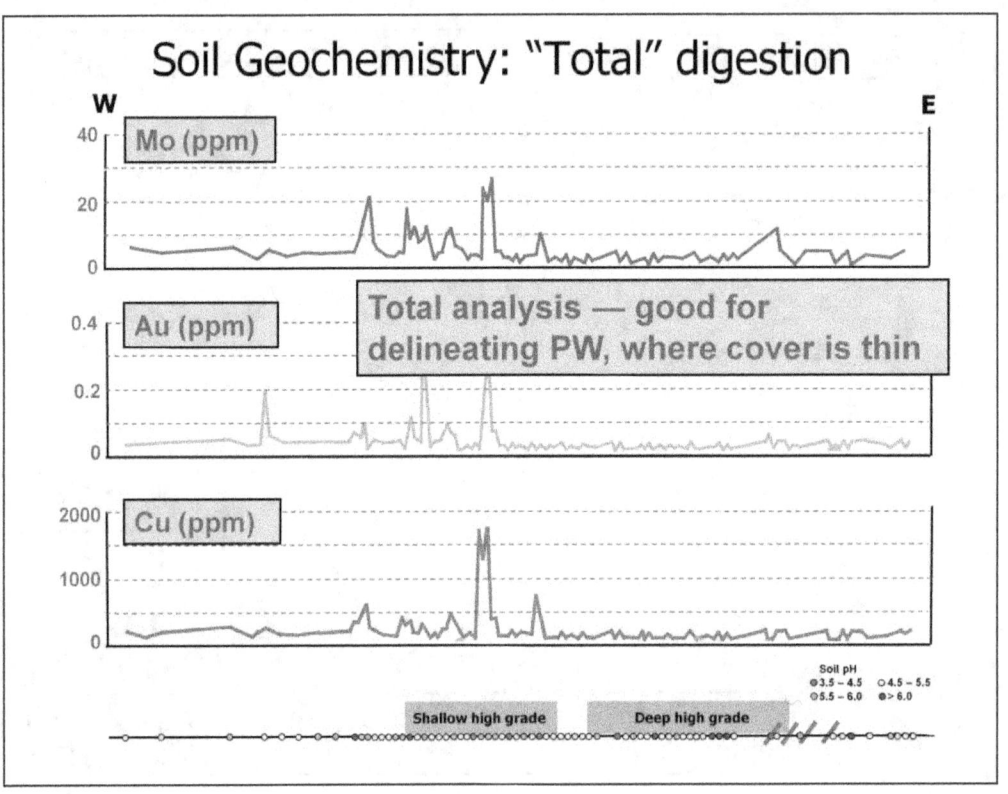

Again, here is Cu in ppm; highest values in soils are 1,830 ppm.

Abundances of elements like Au, As, and Mo show very similar concentration profiles.

The total analyses are likely reflecting the presence of sulfides in the soils.

Total analyses effectively delineate the shallow Pebble West, but not the deeper Pebble East.

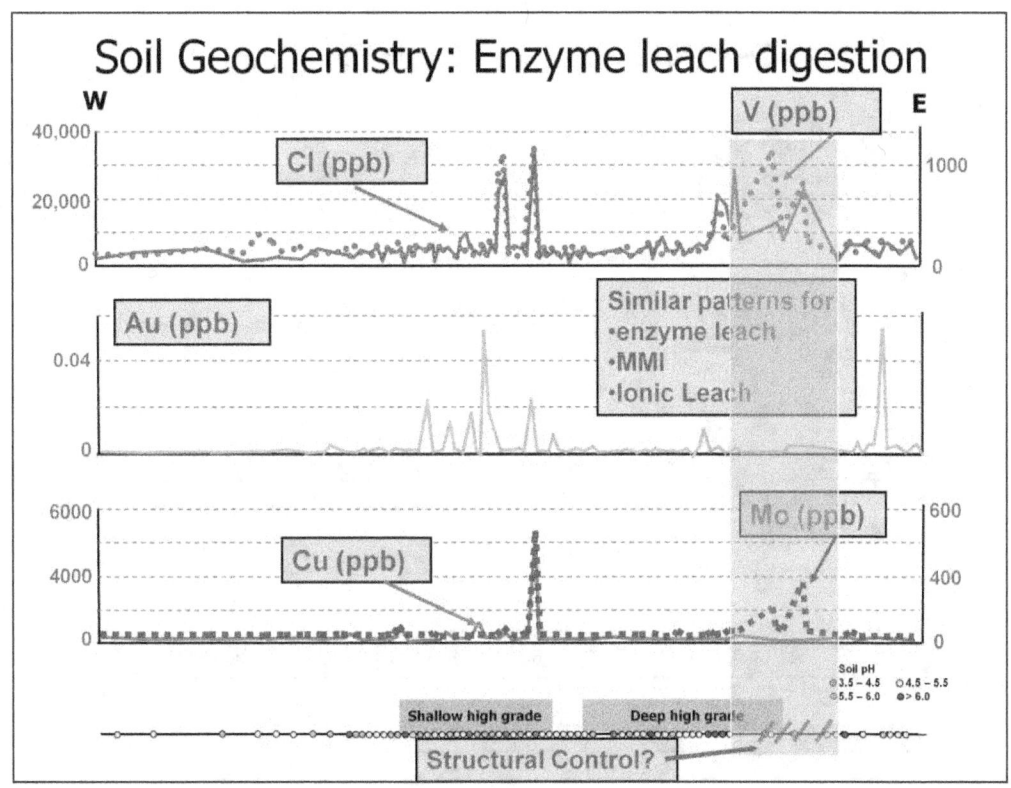

Soil anomalies at Pebble East are adjacent to NE-trending normal faults that define the graben. This may indicate migration of metals via water along faults into Mn and Fe oxides.

Partial leach techniques, such as enzyme leach (shown here), MMI, and Ionic Leach show metal anomalies over the deep Pebble East as well as Pebble West.

The partial leach techniques also suggest some nontraditional pathfinder elements, such as Cl and V that are not typically thought of as exploration tools for porphyry deposits.

Absolute Cl concentrations determined by enzyme leach delineate not only part of Pebble West, but also exhibit a multipoint anomaly associated with graben-bounding faults at Pebble East.

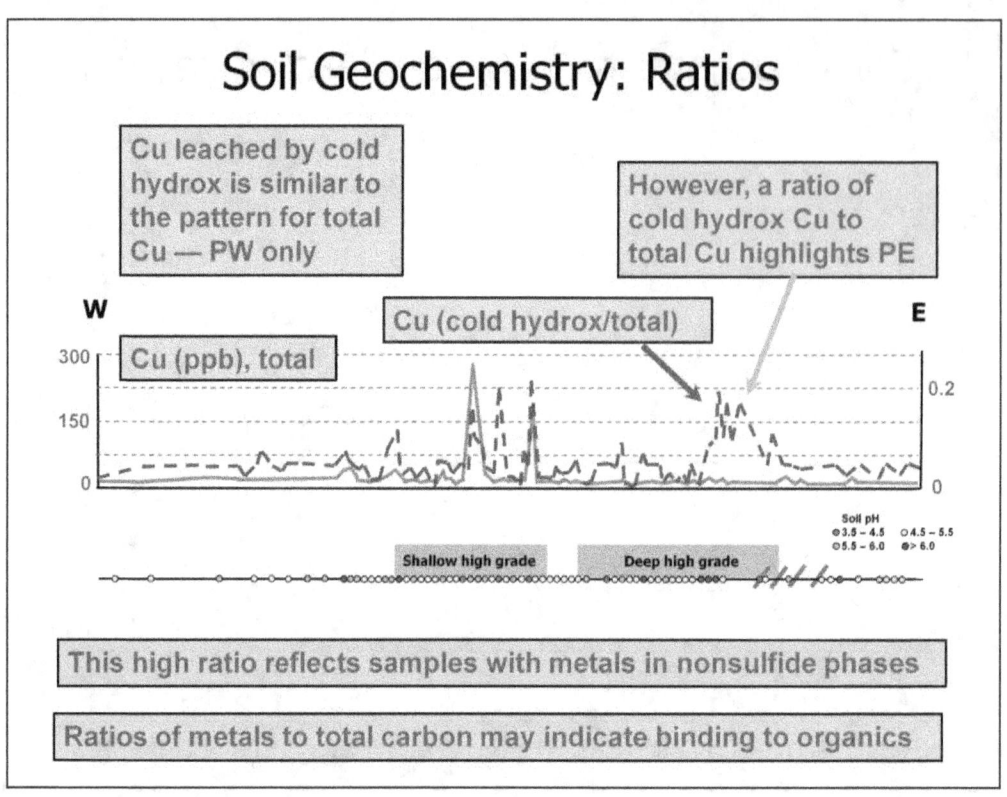

Element ratios also provide some insight. The red line is Cu (total analysis) and identifies Pebble West, but not Pebble East.

Cu leached by cold hydroxylamine shows a similar pattern, highlighting Pebble West only.

However, a ratio of cold hydroxylamine Cu to total Cu highlights Pebble East, reflecting the presence of Cu in nonsulfide phases.

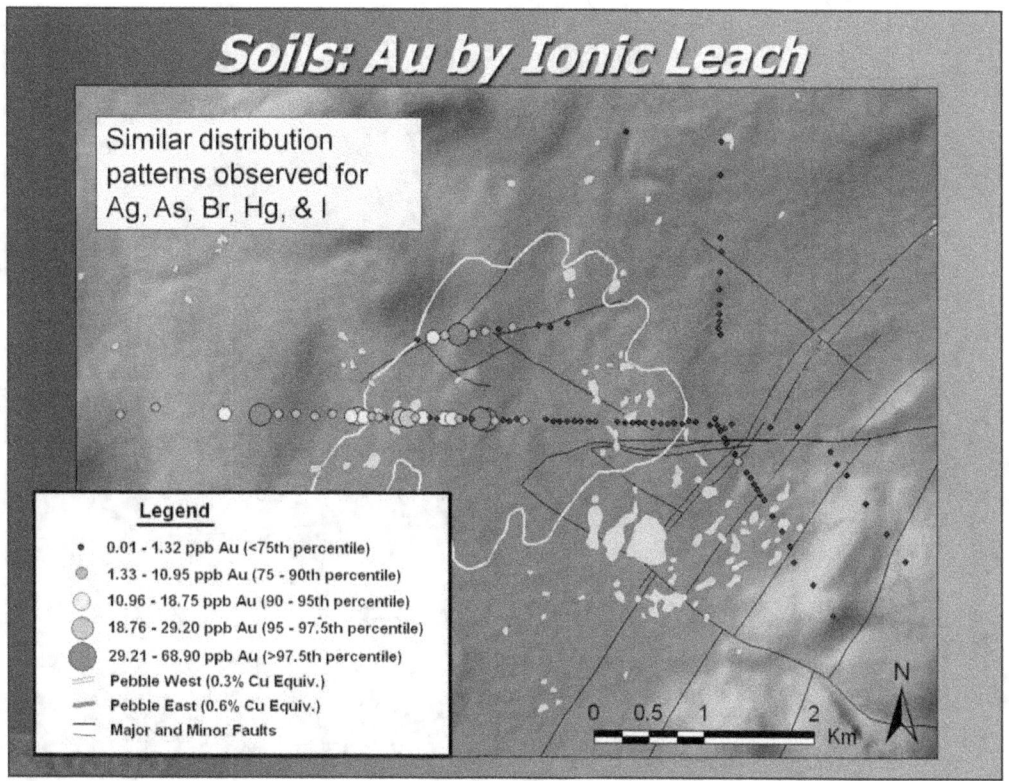

Now I'll show results for a couple elements by the Ionic Leach method.
Pebble West is indicated well by anomalous samples, particularly for Au.
There are similar distributions for Ag, As, Br, Hg, and I concentrations.

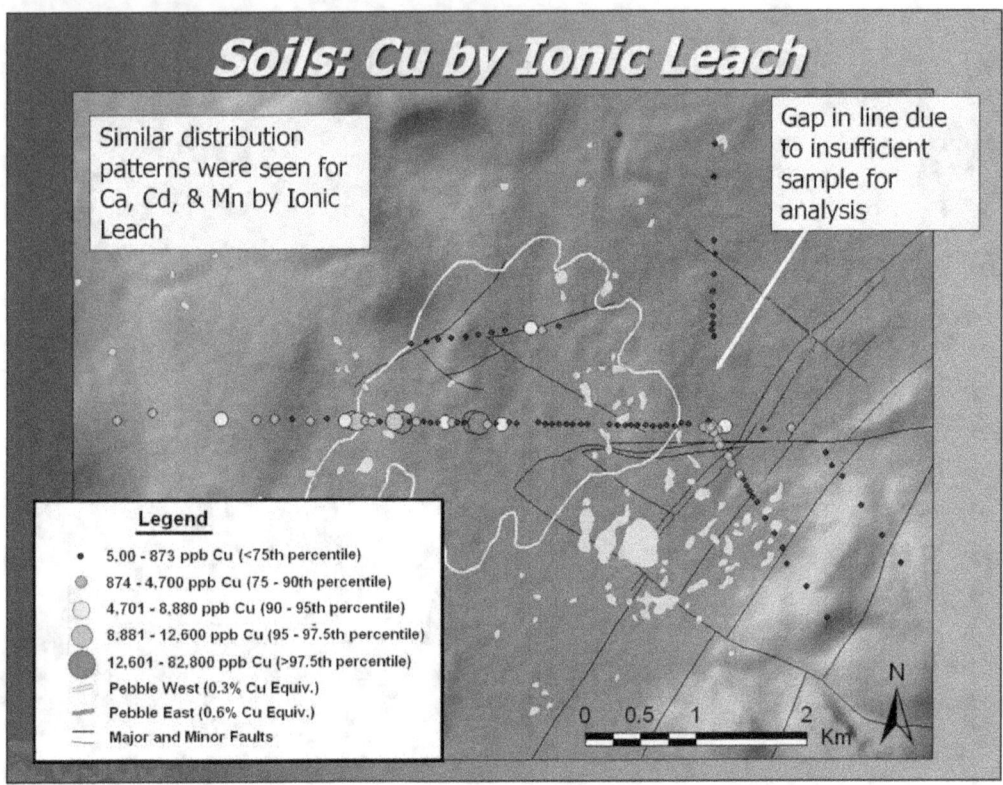

Soils: Cu by Ionic Leach

Similar distribution patterns were seen for Ca, Cd, & Mn by Ionic Leach

Gap in line due to insufficient sample for analysis

Legend
- 5.00 - 873 ppb Cu (<75th percentile)
- 874 - 4,700 ppb Cu (75 - 90th percentile)
- 4,701 - 8,880 ppb Cu (90 - 95th percentile)
- 8,881 - 12,600 ppb Cu (95 - 97.5th percentile)
- 12,601 - 82,800 ppb Cu (>97.5th percentile)
- Pebble West (0.3% Cu Equiv.)
- Pebble East (0.6% Cu Equiv.)
- Major and Minor Faults

0 0.5 1 2 Km

N

Anomalous Cu concentrations by the Ionic Leach method again indicate Pebble West strongly.

The deeper Pebble East also is indicated by several samples overlying the graben-bounding faults.

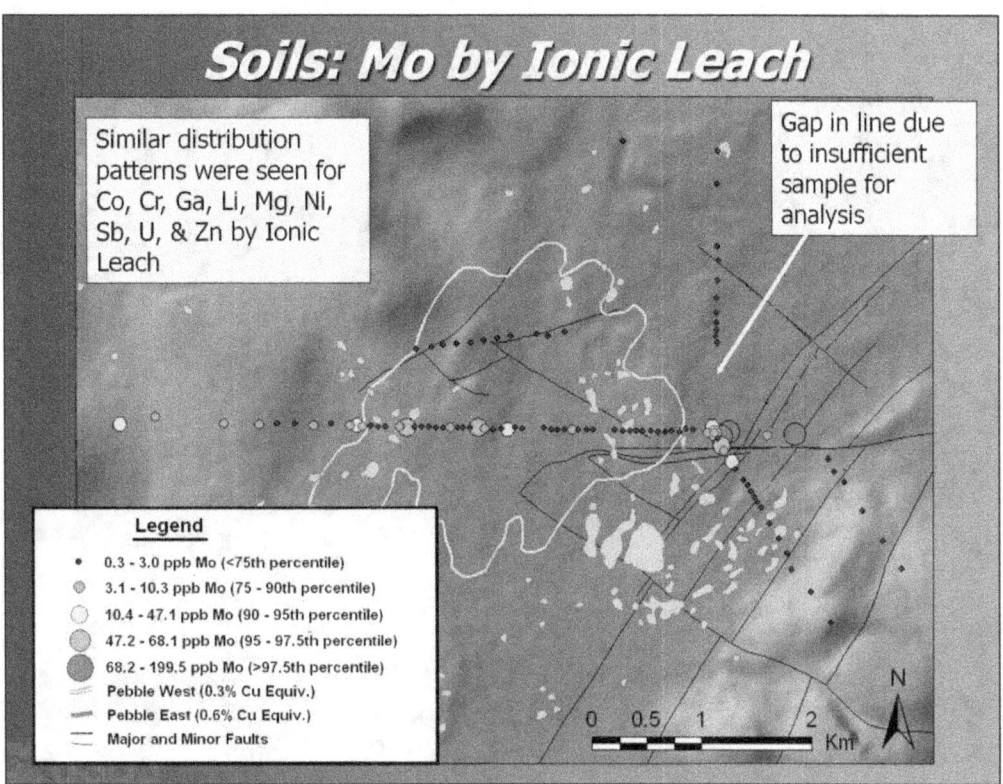

Soils: Mo by Ionic Leach

Similar distribution patterns were seen for Co, Cr, Ga, Li, Mg, Ni, Sb, U, & Zn by Ionic Leach

Gap in line due to insufficient sample for analysis

Legend
- 0.3 - 3.0 ppb Mo (<75th percentile)
- 3.1 - 10.3 ppb Mo (75 - 90th percentile)
- 10.4 - 47.1 ppb Mo (90 - 95th percentile)
- 47.2 - 68.1 ppb Mo (95 - 97.5th percentile)
- 68.2 - 199.5 ppb Mo (>97.5th percentile)
- Pebble West (0.3% Cu Equiv.)
- Pebble East (0.6% Cu Equiv.)
- Major and Minor Faults

0 0.5 1 2 Km

Mo concentrations are highest over Pebble East in samples near the graben-bounding faults.

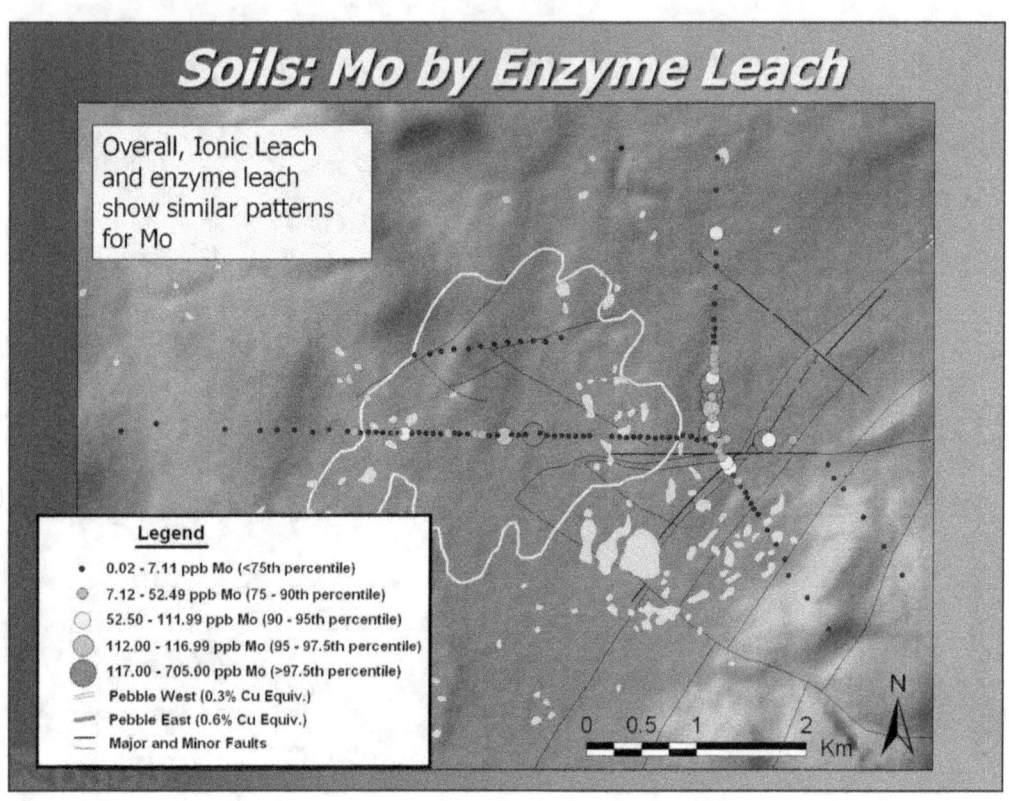

Soils: concluding remarks

- Strong leaches identify shallow mineralized areas at PW while weaker leaches identify the deeper PE deposit

- Multiple leach methods work to varying degrees
  - De-ionized water and Na-pyrophosphate leaches performed poorly

- Graben-bounding faults at PE appear to be conduits for migrating metals from depth to surface soils
  - This agrees with the water data shown earlier

- Significant anomaly patterns at PW and PE found for: Ag, As, Au, Cu, Mo, Re, Sb, Tl, & U

- In addition to these are "nonconventional" pathfinder elements such as Cl and V over both PE and PW

- Several partial leach methods identify the deeper PE, but curiously not always at identical sample sites

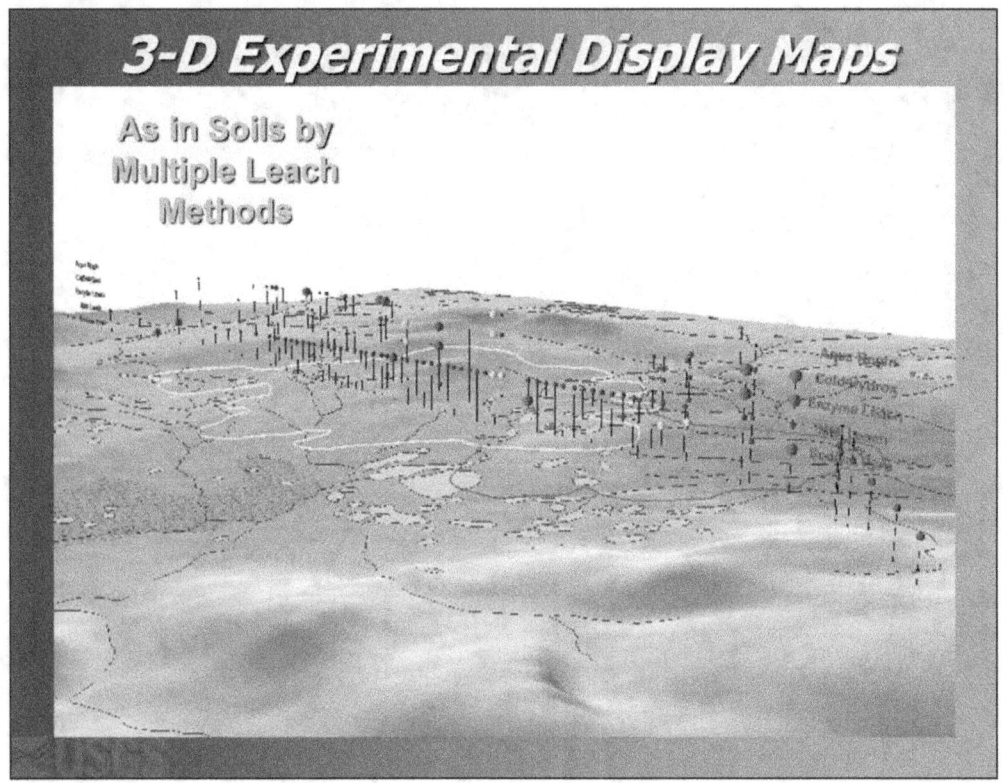

3-D Experimental Display Maps

As in Soils by Multiple Leach Methods

3-D maps are being produced to synthesize and visualize the large amount of data generated from the numerous soil extraction schemes.

This example shows As analyzed by five different partial extraction methods.

View looking NW across deposit.

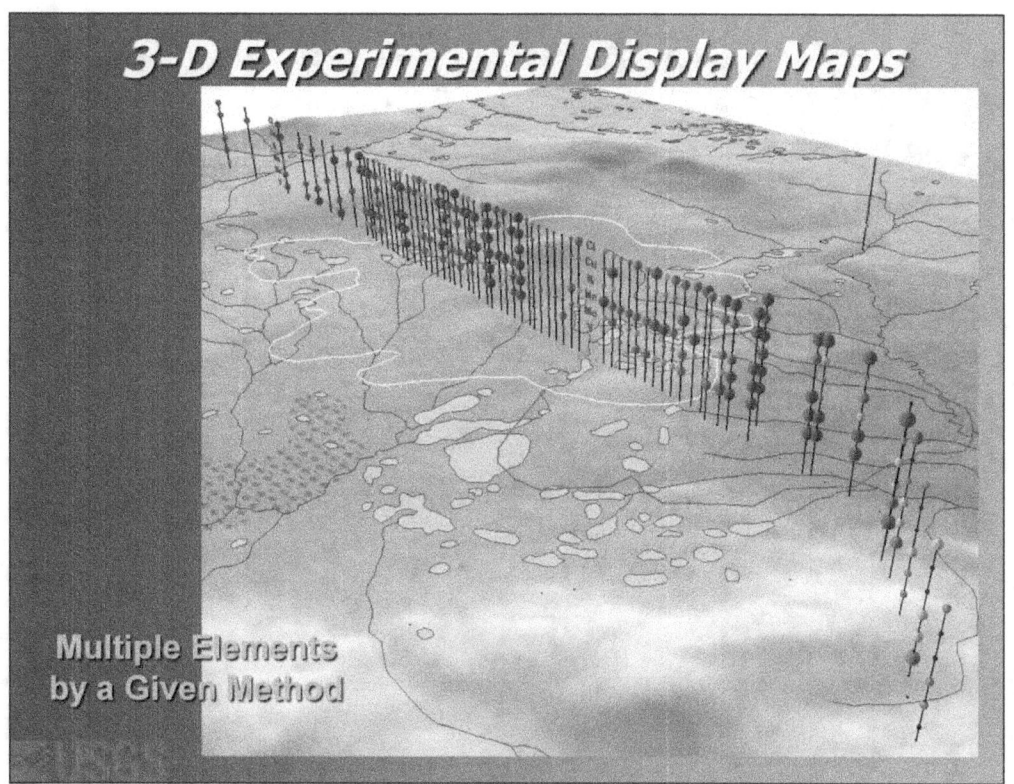

3-D Experimental Display Maps

Multiple Elements by a Given Method

This example shows results for multiple elements analyzed by a single leach method.

View looking NW across deposit.

Mechanisms?

- Periodic pumping of groundwater during seismic events?

- Gas transport?

- Electrochemical transport?
  - Method under investigation using self-potential

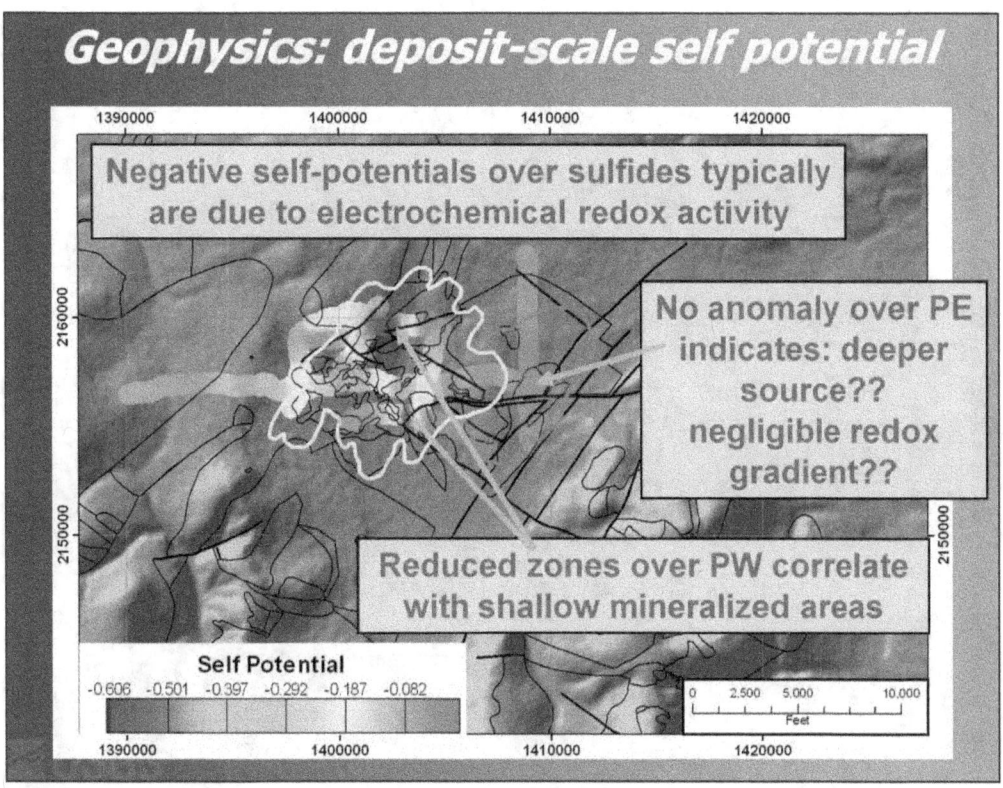

The basic redox transport model is that metals migrate vertically along redox gradients created when a sulfide body oxidizes.

Note reduced zones over center of Pebble West, indicative of shallow mineralized areas.

Note lack of anomaly over Pebble East, reflecting deeper source and/or negligible redox gradient at depth.

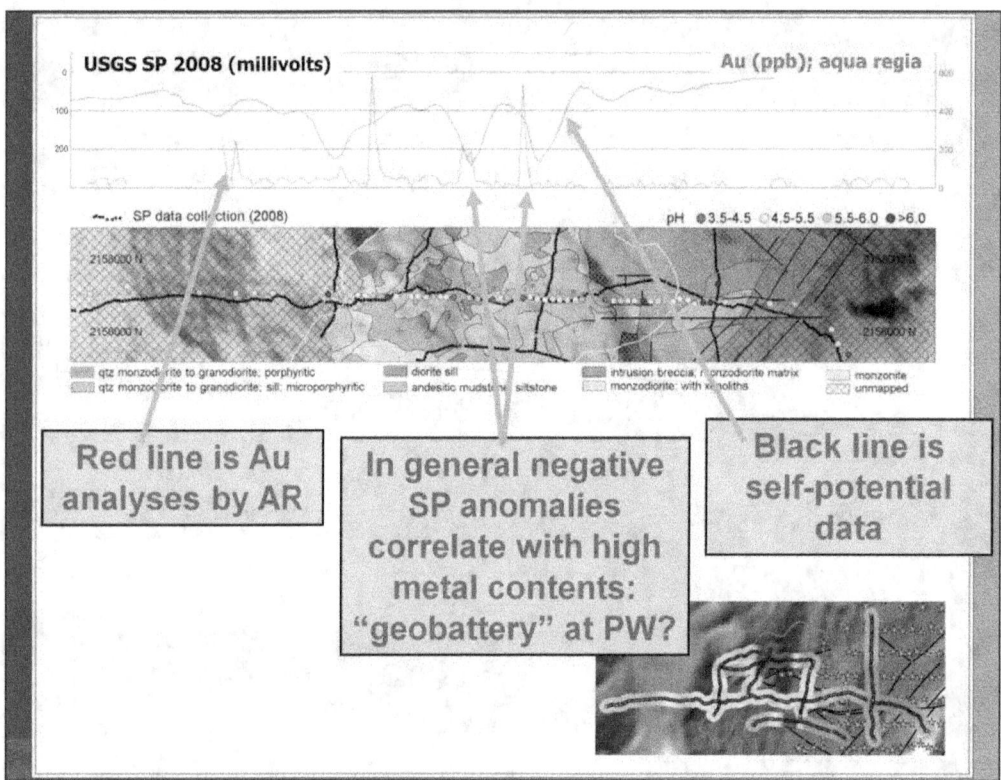

This cross section is similar to those shown earlier for soil geochemistry. In the middle panel, the colored dots show the soil pH along the 2007 soil line. The black lines are the SP survey lines.

The top panel shows the self potential (SP) data in black (as millivolts) versus Au (by partial extraction method, in ppb) in red.

Several large SP anomalies are associated with Pebble West. These negative anomalies are generally negatively correlated with the highest Au contents in the soils.

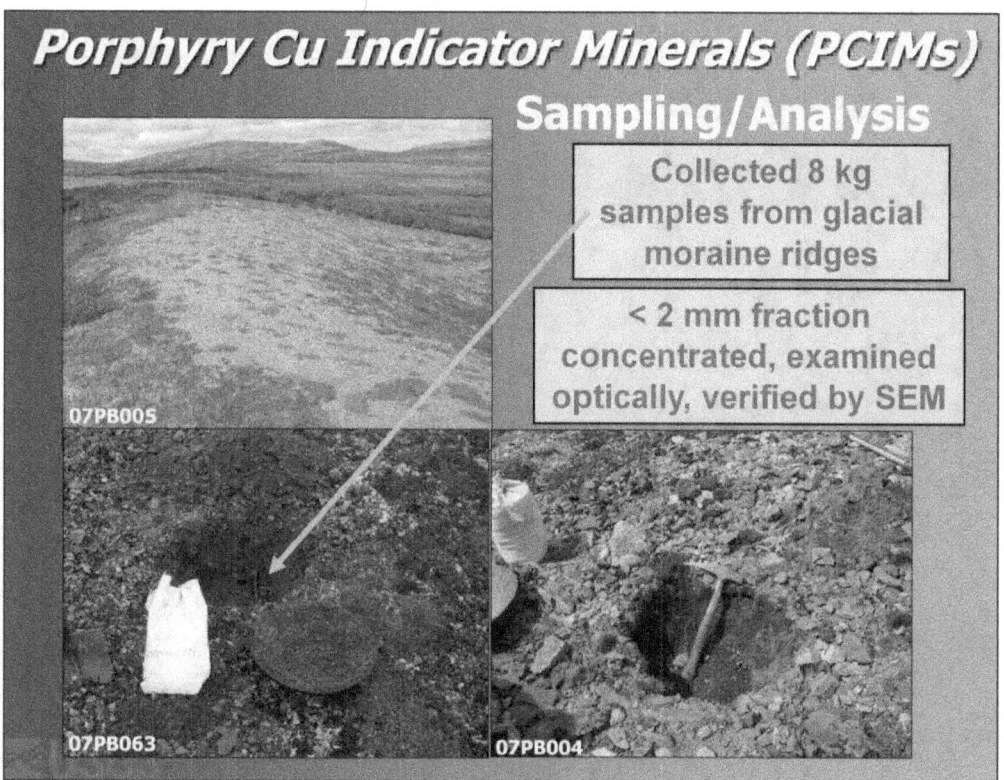

Forty nine glacial till samples were collected between 2007 and 2009 for indicator mineral analysis.

Samples were collected up-ice, through the deposit area, down-ice, and distal to the deposit area.

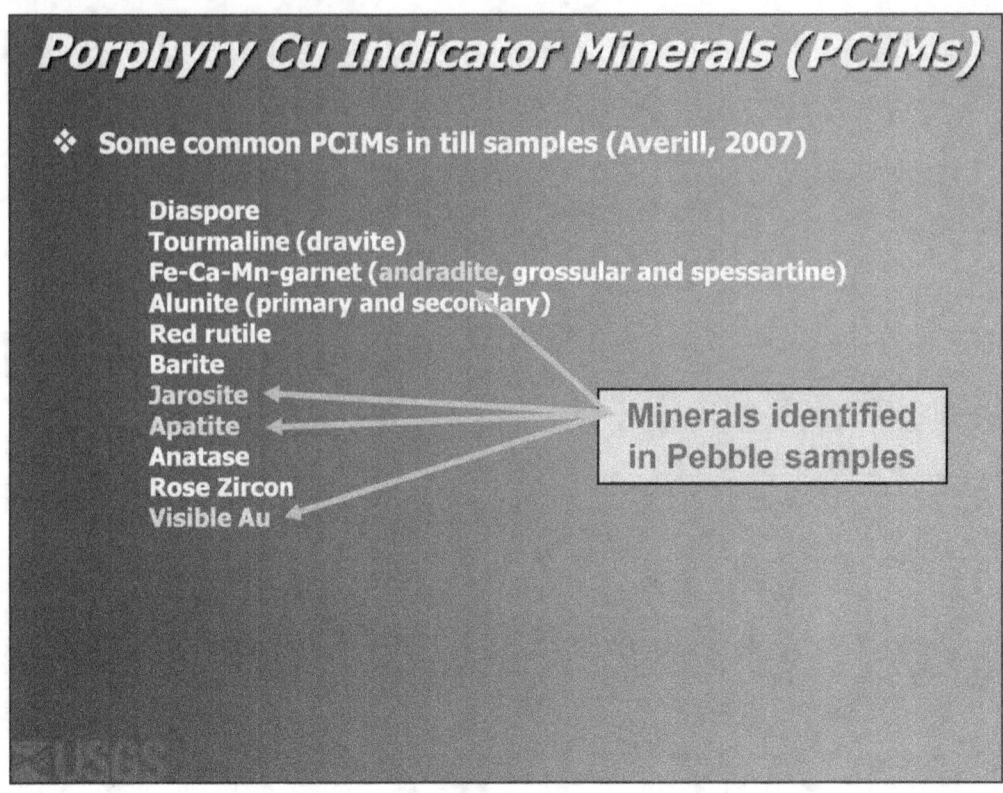

Just four of the common PCIMs were identified in the Pebble area samples.

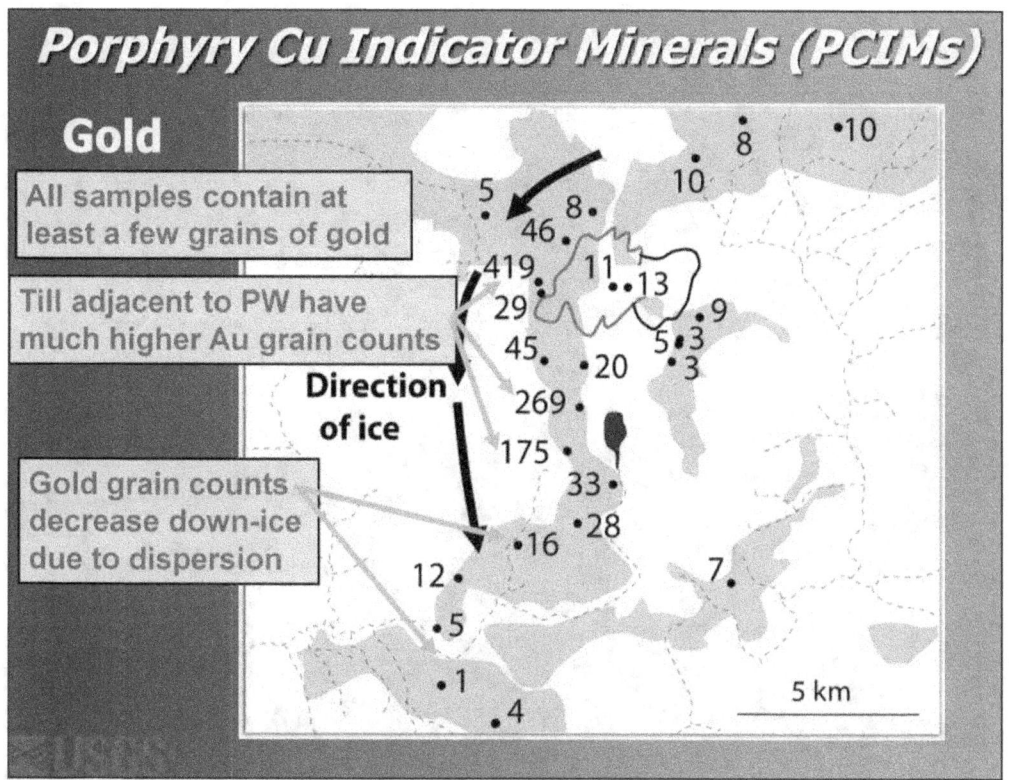

Porphyry Cu Indicator Minerals (PCIMs)

Gold

All samples contain at least a few grains of gold

Till adjacent to PW have much higher Au grain counts

Direction of ice

Gold grain counts decrease down-ice due to dispersion

5 km

There are many possible sources of gold in the region, including porphyry, skarn, and epithermal deposits in the region.

However, the highest concentrations of gold grains are found in tills immediately down–ice of the Pebble deposit.

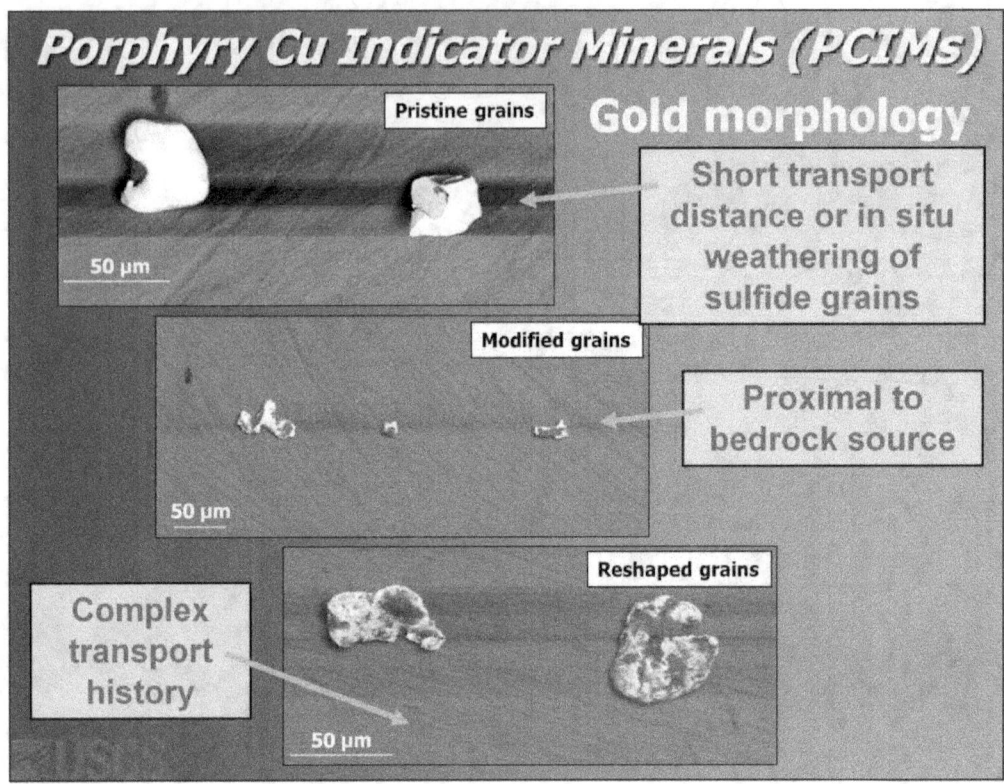

Gold grain morphology is also an important clue.

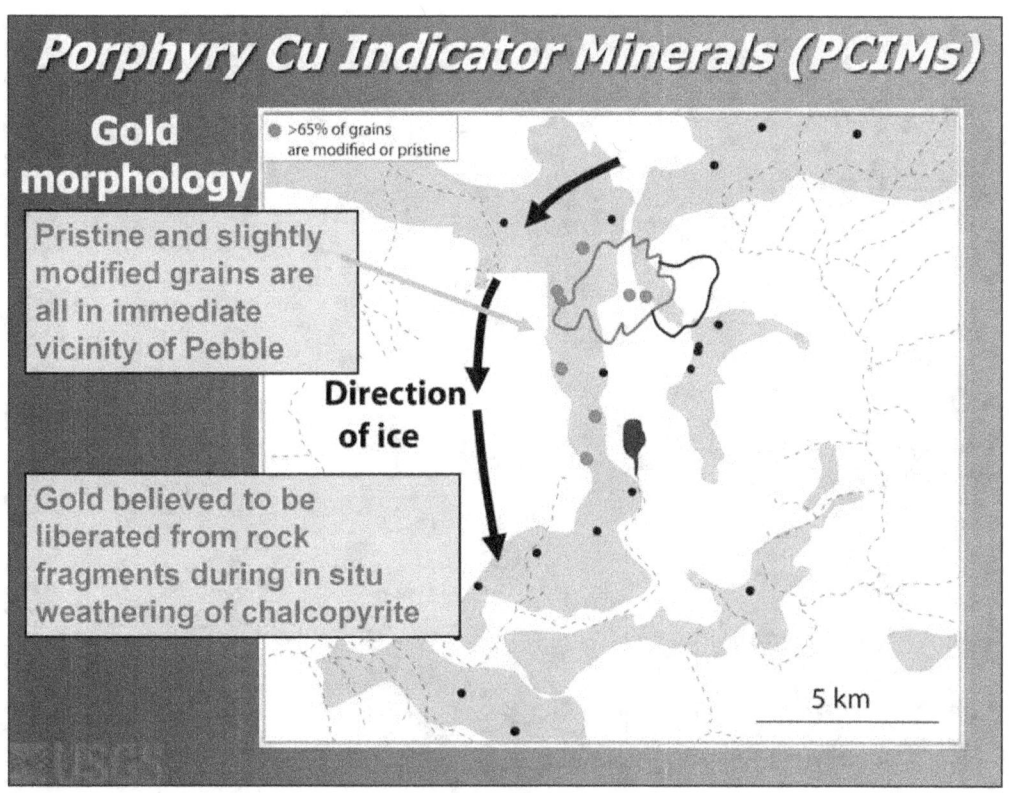

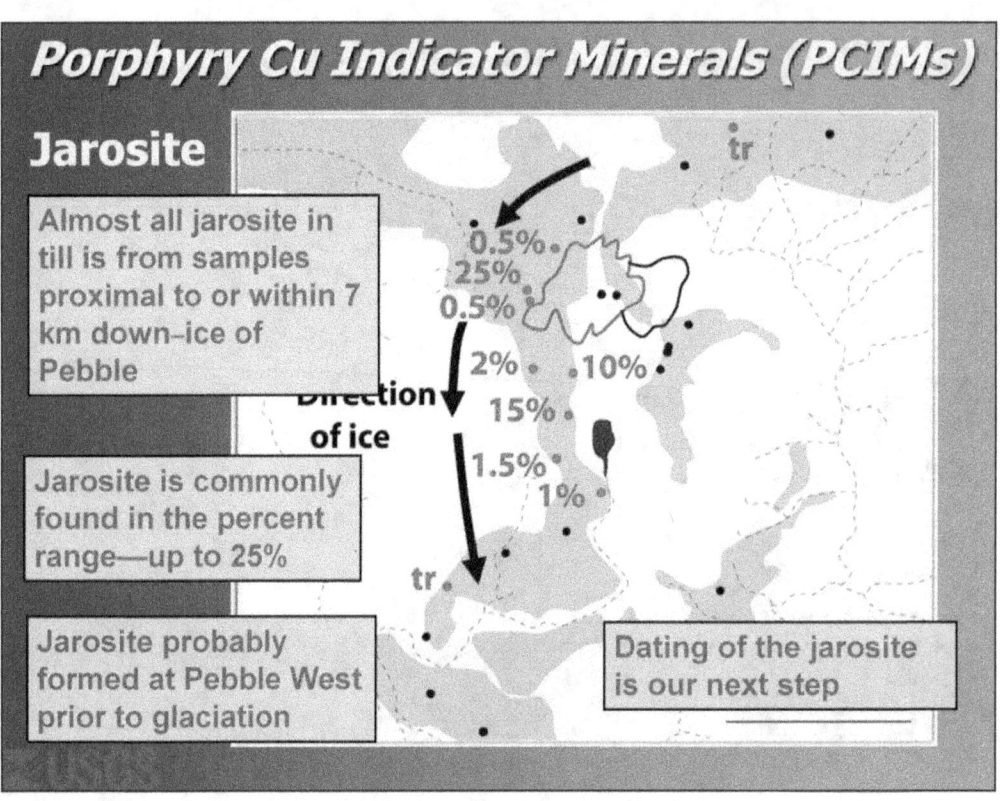

Porphyry Cu Indicator Minerals (PCIMs)

Jarosite

Almost all jarosite in till is from samples proximal to or within 7 km down–ice of Pebble

Jarosite is commonly found in the percent range—up to 25%

Jarosite probably formed at Pebble West prior to glaciation

Direction of ice

Dating of the jarosite is our next step

tr

0.5%
25%
0.5%
2% 10%
15%
1.5%
1%
tr

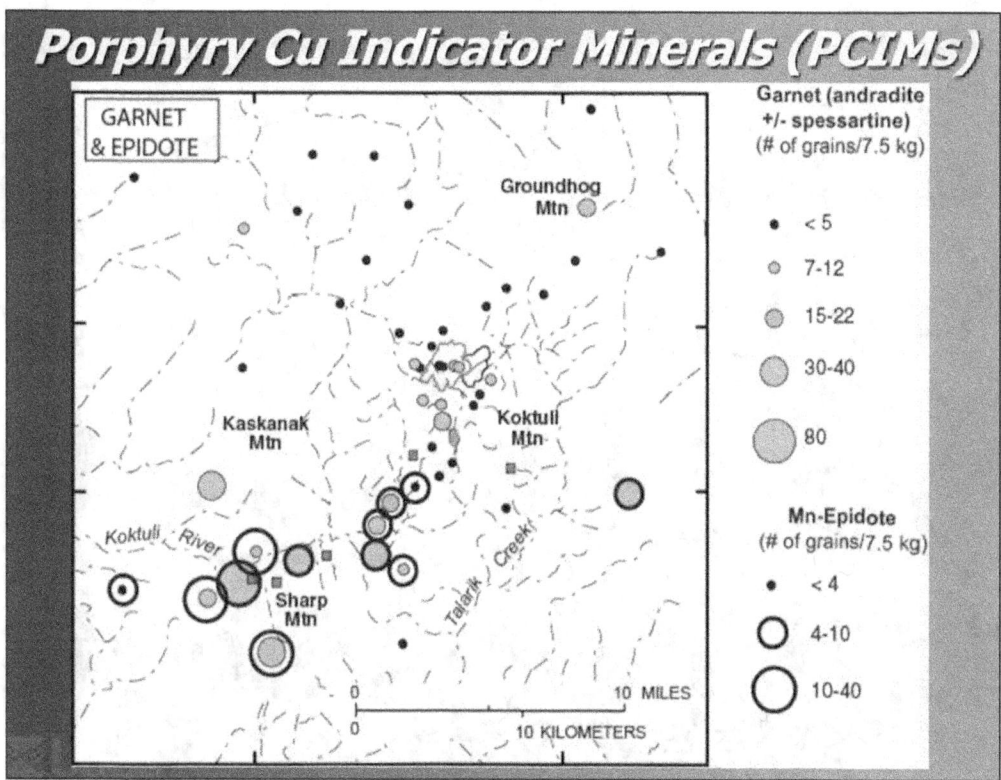

This map shows a broader area around the Pebble deposit than the previous slides. The Pebble deposit is indicated near the center of the map.

Andradite garnet is another known PCIM. Though a few samples have garnet grains down–ice from Pebble, higher garnet grain counts are found in till samples immediately down–ice of skarn and porphyry mineral occurrences in the vicinity of Sharp Mountain. Epidote grain counts show a similar distribution.

Final Conclusions

Regional scale

❖ Water geochemistry (ponds, lakes, streams, seeps) and PCIMs (gold abundance/morphology, jarosite, garnet) in tills are useful to identify broad areas with potential for deposits in SW Alaska

Deposit scale

❖ Soil geochemistry (total metals and strong leaches) delineates shallow mineralized areas; weak partial leaches are promising for detecting deeper deposits in SW Alaska

❖ While not covered here, geophysics (magnetics, gravity? MT?) are useful to highlight structure, depth of cover, and presence of intrusions

    ❖ good for selecting targets for focused geochemistry

USGS

Water, Soil, Sediment Data

- **2007 Raw Data Available**
  - USGS OFR 2008-1132

- **2008 Raw Data Available**
  - USGS OFR 2009-1239

Google:
'Pebble USGS geochemistry'
- Have a few CDs here

Thank You!

≋USGS
science for a changing world

Geochemical Data for Samples Collected
in 2007 Near the Concealed Pebble
Porphyry Cu-Au-Mo Deposit, Southwest
Alaska

By David L. Fey, Matthew Granitto, Stuart A. Giles, Steven M. Smith, Robert G. Eppinger, and Karen D. Kelley

Open-File Report 2008-1132

U.S. Department of the Interior
U.S. Geological Survey

www.ingramcontent.com/pod-product-compliance
Lightning Source LLC
Chambersburg PA
CBHW080438290526
45791CB00008BA/2540